Telling the Truth in Love

Telling the Truth in Love

A Brief History of the
Baptist and Reflector
from 1835

By William Fletcher Allen

Lonnie Wilkey, editor

FIELDS PUBLISHING, INCORPORATED

NASHVILLE, TENNESSEE

Printed in the United States of America

Library of Congress Card Number: 2005935494

ISBN:1-57843-031-3

published by

Fields Publishing Inc.
8120 Sawyer Brown Road, Suite 108
Nashville, TN 37221
615-662-1344
e-mail: tfields@fieldspublishing.com

Contents

Foreword

In late 2004 as I began to look over the production schedule of the *Baptist and Reflector* for 2005, I realized that this year would be the 170th anniversary of the paper. Begun in 1835 as *THE BAPTIST,* the paper has evolved over the years to its current role as the official newsjournal of the Tennessee Baptist Convention.

As I explored ways to honor our past, I originally intended for this book to be a collection of editorials and columns from *B&R* editors over the years. I turned to the paper's only living former editor for his advice. Fletcher Allen is not just my former boss. He is my mentor and most of all, one of my best friends. Part of my intention was to honor not only the paper's past with this publication, but to honor him as well. Fletcher served as editor of the *B&R* for almost eleven years, making him one of the longest tenured editors since the 1960s. I owe him a debt of gratitude for bringing in a young journalist in 1988 who had no prior experience on a Baptist State paper staff. His tutelage helped me grow and mature as a Baptist journalist, and I was honored and humbled when the Search Committee for the *Baptist and Reflector* chose me to be his successor in 1998.

He agreed to take an active part in the publication. Quite frankly, this book would not be published had it not been for him. He worked tirelessly, putting in untold hours on this project. Because of Fletcher's deep love for history and the paper itself, the book soon evolved to become a brief history, not just a collection of editorials.

As Fletcher states in the Prologue, this book is not a comprehensive history, but it is a beginning point. Other than special issues of the paper commemorating key anniversaries, there has never been a written history of the *Baptist and Reflector.*

We trust our readers and others will enjoy this compilation of our past. The basis for the title of this book comes from a Bible verse often used as a motto by several editors. "Telling the truth in love" is a phrase derived from Ephesians 4:15 ("... speaking [telling] the truth in love, we will in all things grow up into Him who is the head, that is, Christ" NIV). It speaks of unity in the body of Christ and Christian growth.

I want to express appreciation to several others who played major roles in the publication of *Telling the Truth in Love*.

First, I want to thank many of Fletcher Allen's friends and family members who contributed to help make this publication possible. The majority of this book is funded by special contributions.

I also want to thank the current staff of the *Baptist and Reflector* — Connie Davis Bushey, Susie Edwards, Mary Nimmo, Betty Williams, and Marcia Knox. Each one played a role in helping to produce the book. Special thanks also goes to Royce DeGrie of the design services staff of the Tennessee Baptist Convention for his cover design and to Tim Fields and Fields Publishing for their work as publisher.

I also want to thank faithful readers of the *Baptist and Reflector*. Without you, there would be no paper. For 170 years the *Baptist and Reflector* has been a faithful servant to Tennessee Baptists. My prayer is that the paper will continue to play a major role in our convention as we "tell the story of Tennessee Baptists."

Lonnie Wilkey, editor
Baptist and Reflector
October 2005

Prologue:
The Editor's Desk

Ask your school children — some will say history is dull, just a bunch of names, dates, and places. Well, welcome to a fresh look-history that debunks that idea. History is neither dull, nor only a record of nondescript facts that make no contribution to the intelligent mind. Read on. We have a different kind of history for you, one that stirs imagination, and begs the question, what if...? Put together names, dates, and places, and add some verbs and adjectives — and it's history.

Pull up your chair to the Editor's Desk. This is where the editor prays, plans, and produces. As we sit at The Desk and look back, you and I will be involved in history! I have been there — now it's your turn.

We'll attempt to bring some *Baptist and Reflector* history out of the shadows — into our world. Get ready for an adventure story with unsung heroes. The paper itself is history as it conveys thoughts, plans, ideas, events, decisions, and forums for ordinary Baptists. The words became stories of God's people at work. So this history compels because it tells us who we are and from whence we came, as Baptists. Historical calendar dates are important, but the emphasis of the *B&R* story is more than dates.

I want readers to see the paper as the editors see it. Understand the editors as people with a love for Baptists, and a willingness to give their lives in service. We share something of the editors' personalities, without digging deeply into political and doctrinal issues. Each editor is different, and some came to the post with special interests.

I am privileged to be a part of this project. During my years as *B&R* editor, I admired the paper's strength and character, and its role in ongoing Convention life. I wondered why the history had never been written. This book attempts to tell something of that heritage. Beginning with Richard Owen, I've known the recent editors. These connections helped in writing, but for the others, research was the only source. Each chapter is unique, not only in personalities, but also in the approach.

Editors of the paper always have believed in missions, evangelism, our colleges, and other institutions and agencies — and most had a vital part by serving on committees and boards. It's easy to forget that editors are people. They are more than reporters — they are encouragers, supporters, and caretakers.

There are unknowns. Everything was not written down. What were the editors like? Where did the editors get newsprint for printing? Did they have good relations with the post offices? How did they deal with advertisers? Who served with the editors? What about difficulties with transportation? How did they authenticate news items without modern communications? How did they relate to convention leaders? How did editors and publishers deal with so many consolidations with other papers? We can answer only some of these questions because of limited time and dearth of space.

Early in the research process, I found confirming evidence that the paper owns a vital place in the history of the Tennessee Baptist Convention. It was necessary to follow closely the paper's trail, and at the same time, to avoid being swept up with every Convention action or controversy. I also noticed one peculiarity in names — for years there was a trend for editors and other leaders to use initials in place of given names. I used their whole names and initials interchangeably. (Frequently the paper's official name was shortened to the familiar initials, *B&R*.)

James L. Sullivan, Southern Baptist leader and statesman for many years, knew more about Tennessee Baptists and their history than did most historians. He often was called "Mr. Baptist," and served as president of the Baptist Sunday School Board (LifeWay Christian Resources), Nashville, for twenty-two years. In particular, Sullivan had a passion for Baptist history. He knew the value of the *Baptist and Reflector* as Tennessee Baptists' newsjournal. A classic Sullivanism explains a good definition:

"I view history not as a memorization of dates and happenings appearing static like a monument. Rather I see history as people and the crises they face daily, flowing like a river in which every drop of rain fuses with all other raindrops and moves on with each effected by the other. ... W.O. Carver at Southern Baptist Theological Seminary taught me to appreciate history rather than hold to its jumbled-up parts. And we must know where we came from before we can understand who we are."

Bravo, Mr. Baptist! That's a good portrait of Tennessee Baptists. The history of churches and organizations, personal and family lives, events all around us, also flows like that river of raindrops and tributaries, each affected by the other. And this is how we should look at ourselves. Any other way distorts reality and robs us of the tremendous gift of knowing our heritage.

In this 170th anniversary year of the paper's founding, the *Baptist and Reflector* remains a voice for truth and an advocate of the people. Born in Nashville, the paper was the child of Robert Boyte Crawford Howell, the "brand new" pastor of First Baptist Church. He wanted the paper to be a messenger to the people, spokesman for the people, and conveyor of all the news they needed.

Taking Sullivan's advice, I've tried to avoid the "jumbled up parts."

Let's return to the beginning. In January 1835, just a few weeks after arriving in Nashville from Virginia with his family, Howell published the first edition of *THE BAPTIST*, forerunner of our *Baptist and Reflector*. The title was in bold capital letters, with an emphatic period (.). He made a statement. It was the first Baptist newspaper in Tennessee. On the front page of that baby newsjournal, Howell made plain his objectives, and the purpose of the paper. You'll find in this book a reproduced copy of that page. And you can read more about it in the first chapter.

The paper had only three editors during its first eighty-two years. Howell, along with James R. Graves and Edgar E. Folk, served a mostly uninformed body of believers. A contentious atmosphere during those years hindered growth and unity. The editors and their problems and situations are a necessary part of the entire story. From the beginning, Howell's paper attempted to fulfill its role. There is evidence of a growing reputation of fairness and clarity. Look at this example.

Among the letters of congratulations to the paper for its 140th anniversary edition in 1975, was this note from Porter Routh, then executive secretary-treasurer of the Southern Baptist Convention's Executive Committee:

"Ten years before the invention of the rotary printing press,

11

The desk used by four editors of the Baptist and Reflector — *James Lester, Al Shackleford, Wm. Fletcher Allen, and Lonnie Wilkey.*

Tennessee Baptists were receiving a crudely printed journal which not only served as a guide book in the development of spiritual truth, but also as a chronicle of historical events in those early days.

"During these 140 years, the *Baptist and Reflector* has continued to be 'looked for' by Baptists of the Volunteer State, and today it is providing an enlarging service and greater inspiration as it is 'speaking the truth in love'."

In researching the story of the *B&R*, many sources were examined, including books, papers, and pamphlets. I interviewed several Tennessee Baptists who had *B&R* connections. We are indebted to all who gave assistance. Four books have been most helpful: W. Fred Kendall's *A History of the Tennessee Baptist Convention, 1974; Tennessee Baptists, a Comprehensive History, 1779-1999, by Albert Wardin, 1999; Contending for the Right to Know, A History of the Southern Baptist Press Association 1895-1995,* by C. William Junker, 1996; and *Road to Augusta,* Joe W. Burton, 1976. I referred to another book for some quotes on crises — *Not a Silent People,* by Walter B. Shurden, 1972. Bound volumes of the paper and miscellaneous copies were extremely helpful. Records kept in the TBC archives in Brentwood helped verify information. I'm pleased to endorse the books mentioned, and encourage readers to explore them.

Here are the names and years of service for those who followed Howell, Graves, and Folk — Albert R. Bond, 1917-1920; Murphy R. Cooper, Hight C. Moore, J.D. Moore, and O.E. Bryan, covered 1920-25; John D. Freeman, 1925-33; O.W. Taylor, 1933-50; Richard N. Owen, 1950-68; James A. Lester, 1968-73; Eura Lannom, 1973-76 (acting); Alvin Shackleford, 1976-87; Charlie Warren, 1987 (acting); Wm. Fletcher Allen, 1987-98; Lonnie H. Wilkey, 1998 —. [Editor Alvin Shackleford, in a definitive editorial of August 1985, discussing "the purpose of the *Baptist and Reflector*", stated that E.E. Folk, J.R. Graves, and J.B. Moody were listed as editors in the August 29, 1889 issue].

Special editions tell us of celebrations of anniversaries — a centennial issue of sixty-four pages edited by O.W. Taylor, Richard Owen's paper noting the 125th anniversary, Alvin Shackleford's honoring the paper for its 150th birthday; and in 1995, the 160th was celebrated.

From its birth in 1835 as *THE BAPTIST*, the paper has been its unwavering call for freedom of the press. The editors, coming from different levels of experience, recognized their responsibility to "trust the Lord and tell the people." From handset type to sophisticated computerized efficiency, they managed not only to survive, but also to tell the story. Though they struggled with lack of funding, hard times and wars, doctrinal and scriptural disputes, through the years they firmly established a good reputation for the paper. They knew that churches and people, in order to make good decisions, needed the news. And personal views frequently revealed some bias.

The paper's struggle to build readership and financial support was difficult. Things haven't changed much since then. Circulation increased during the paper's first eighty years — partly because of Convention controversy, since the paper was the only printed source for such somewhat up-to-date news. The highest level of readers came during the years of Owen, Lannom, and Shackleford with about 82,000 subscribers. Friction, spawned by unending controversies, prompted other papers and newsletters to crop up, and claim some readers in the 1987 — present

13

era. Circulation has hovered around 50,000 since the mid-1980s. I believe you've opened this book because you are interested — now step back into history. The story of the *Baptist and Reflector* will fascinate you, the reader, with humor, pathos, good times and bad, and reality of news. Without all the news, ordinary and extraordinary, life becomes dull. Remember the river of history? We are part of it, even as we view things from the Editor's Desk.

Walter B. Shurden, noted Southern Baptist historian and professor, in penning a pamphlet for the former Historical Commission of the SBC, cited major crises that shaped Southern Baptist life.

He listed the crisis involving missions, the racial crisis, and the Landmark crisis, among others. *Baptist and Reflector* editors dealt with these according to the times. Sometimes editors contributed to the discord. Other crises could be mentioned — such as financial problems, lack of leadership, and political types.

The history of Tennessee's *Baptist and Reflector* combines reality of life — a gallery with photographs, littered with news, and becoming a redemptive force for the present and teacher for the future. As I said before, the story is an amazing adventure. The river of words over these 170 years provides an exciting and liberating journey. If books or newspapers could be heroes, you're reading about one now.

In an historical move outside the comfort of Tennessee Baptist life, E.E. Folk, editor from 1889-1917, became the "father" of the Southern Baptist Press Association (SBPA), a fellowship organization for Baptist editors. He was one who believed such a group would be beneficial for Baptist papers and the editors. It grew more professional through the years, providing workshops and exchange of ideas. Members agreed in recent years to change the name to Association of State Baptist Papers. This group brought together editors of the State Baptist papers. It proved to be a valuable means for discussions and problems solving. *Baptist and Reflector* editors who have been president of the group include — Folk, 1903; John Freeman, 1930-33; O.W. Taylor, 1938 and 1948; Richard Owen, 1961; Alvin Shackleford, 1980; Fletcher Allen, 1992; and Lonnie Wilkey, 2004.

Note two other items worthy of reading and preserving, but too lengthy for this book. Both appear in C. William Junker's history of SBPA, *Contending for the Right to Know.* Folk's editorial, Shall

Southern Baptists Divide? (*B&R*, January 9, 1899) is a classic plea for peace and cooperation among Southern Baptists. The second item is a definitive report on the denominational press given to the SBC in 1901. In it a committee persuasively explained the credibility and value of state papers. The committee was chaired by J.B. Cranfill, first editor of the Texas *Baptist Standard* and first president of the SBPA. Both prophetic pieces can be read in entirety in Junker's book.

The path followed by the *Baptist and Reflector* from its beginning has a few bends and inexplicable turns. Many other Baptist papers and editors are involved as tributaries to the river referred to by James L. Sullivan. Also there is some confusion about dates, but I've tried to focus on the most reliable sources. When editors of faraway past were on the scene, they were producing a paper — perhaps with little concern for historical records.

Typographical mistakes left uncorrected in a later edition may cause some errors. The most accurate record usually is found in bound volumes, though, believe it or not, even editors make an occasional mistake. Handwriting is fallible and typing skills are imperfect! Some of these priceless volumes are tattered and crumbling, some are missing. When in doubt, I have tried to use more than one available source for verification.

Here's a bit of history worth storing in a safe place, but easy to find when it is needed. Minutes of the November 1918 Tennessee Baptist Convention records a committee report on Denominational Literature. It included a succinct definition of the role of Baptist papers — "The real worth of denominational literature is estimated by a proper consideration of the good that it accomplishes through the information given to the people." Albert Bond, *B&R* editor, was one of three messengers who discussed the report. Thank you, Brother Editor!

I'm deeply grateful for the opportunity to serve with three State Baptist papers — South Carolina, Maryland/Delaware, and especially Tennessee, for thirty-two years. And this book has been written and published with stellar assistance from the *Baptist and Reflector* staff — Editor Lonnie Wilkey, Connie Davis Bushey, Susie Edwards, Mary Nimmo, Betty Williams, and Marcia Knox; plus support from other friends of history. Betty Williams has worked with the paper for forty-six years, probably a record tenure for the TBC Executive Board. All have my deepest gratitude.

Today, in the year 2005, the paper follows its own history, always zealous for serving the Lord.

Paul the Apostle said it this way — "Never be lacking in zeal, but keep your spiritual fervor, serving the Lord." — Romans 12:11 (NIV). In this book you, the reader, can dig into some interesting stories.

Now that you're comfortable in your chair at The Editor's Desk, read along with me. Enjoy the trip.

Wm. Fletcher Allen
Franklin, Tennessee
October 2005

CHAPTER ONE

Breaking Barriers
R.B.C. Howell
1835-47

It was 1835, and the United States of America was only sixty years old. The Thirteen Colonies had thrown off British shackles and gained sovereignty. Doors opened for expansion and exploring. A new nation was growing up. Bold, brave ideas were abroad in the land. History was in the making, history that would impact the nation and perhaps the world.

Moreover, the printed words of denominations were beginning to play a major role in shaping that history. It was then that Robert Boyte Crawford Howell started something big, worthy, lasting. Moving from Virginia to Nashville, Tennessee, Howell answered the call to lead a struggling First Baptist Church, and to start a Baptist newspaper.

Howell already had plans for the paper before he and his family arrived in Nashville. Inspired, dedicated, and determined, the dogged pastor did not waste time. Just a few weeks after settling, he published the first edition of the new paper. It was dated January 1, 1835, and he named it *THE BAPTIST*. With that accomplished, he established a place for those who would follow in his path, a road made easier for them.

He saw that the major limitation of church growth was lack of communication. There was no method of supplying potential readers with news and status of other churches. The lands west of Middle Tennessee were unsettled in many ways. This was the Southwest, and Howell wanted to help evangelize the area. His answer? Give them a newspaper!

His energy and passion propelled Howell into the limelight. His desire to bring Baptist churches together was strong. His was the original Baptist paper in Tennessee, and the 2005 model — the *Baptist and Reflector* has a solid foundation. Howell knew the people needed a paper and plunged into the task with grit and wisdom. He wanted Baptists to work together. He also became one of the leaders and founding fathers of the Southern Baptist Convention, which was formed in 1845 in Augusta, Georgia.

David McCullough, noted author and historian, said this about history: "In writing about history or biography, you must remember that nothing was ever on a track. Things could have gone any way at any point. As soon as you say, 'was,' it seems to fix on an event in the past. But nobody ever lived in the past, only in the present.

"The difference is that it was their present. They were just as alive and full of ambition, fear, hope, all the emotions of life. And just like us, they didn't know how it would turn out.

"The challenge is to get the reader beyond thinking that things had to be the way they turned out and to see the ranges of possibilities of how it could have been otherwise."

R.B.C. Howell, Early Years

Howell and those who followed him learned that producing a denominational newspaper is rewarding, but difficult. When he came to Nashville, a community of about 6,000, only a few members were to be found in the decimated First Baptist Church. Those few were discouraged, disorganized, and divided. Howell was prepared for the hard work ahead. He launched a well-written and constructive paper. Those first readers must have been surprised and elated at this conveyor of Baptist news. It was a light in a previously dark arena.

In the May 2, 1935, Centennial issue of the *Baptist and Reflector*, J.H. Grime wrote of the enthusiasm of the church group over Howell's arrival: "He secured a public building with ample room for his first appointment and posted the announcement. It spread like wildfire. Curiosity and other interests brought out an overflow crowd. The circumstances gave the preacher extra power, and he held his audience spellbound for one hour. The few Baptists went away happy and encouraged, while the renegades were chagrined, and the better element much interested." Within two years, the popularity of the paper enabled Howell to publish two issues each month, and the church was awakened. The impact was felt well beyond Nashville.

The editor himself referred to potential problems on the front page of his first THE BAPTIST. Noting his inexperience as an editor, he said he had many fears and misgivings because of the lack of order in the churches, and dissensions and conflict of opinion on doctrinal and other church matters.

Assessing the situation, he realized there had been no churches (certainly none strong enough to continue) in the city until 1820 when First Church Nashville was formed. He knew that eight years later, the church had been taken over, including the building, by dissidents (Campbellites), and was not reorganized until 1830. Howell led the church in a great building program and restored the solid reputation it once had had. So when Howell moved to Nashville in answer to the call for help, he also planned to launch a Baptist newspaper that would spread the good news, the gospel message of Jesus Christ.

On the front page of that first edition, Howell also laid out his plans and reasons for beginning an enterprise that, without cooperation from the churches, would fail. Evidently he believed that a Baptist newspaper would be the best method for informing and inspiring the entire region. Probably every editor who followed Howell would read that page many times, and would feel its influence.

He was convinced that the Southwest (states west of the Southern states), was a strategic area for missions and evangelization.

Howell produced a prospectus, but was not satisfied. In the first paper he wrote, "The first number of THE BAPTIST, we have, at length, laid before our readers. We confess that we do not, without many fears and misgivings, enter the Editorial field. The peculiarly disoriented state of the Church, throughout a large portion of this commonwealth, and many other parts of the great valley of the West, growing, as we believe, out of the prevalence of intestine dissensions, the conflict of opinion, on doctrinal, as well as practical religion ... the skill we might bring would be sufficiently limited."

Howell added that he was inexperienced in "editorial tactics," perhaps sensing discord among denominations and the frequency with which editors quarreled with each other. He said he was not experienced "to sit upon the whirlwind and manage the storm, which now rages in the moral world, we tremble lest we should not be able to accomplish all the good which it is desirable *THE BAPTIST* to effect."

In that editorial, Howell wrote, "... the field before us is large and white unto harvest. For wisdom and strength to cast in the sickle and reap, our confidence is in the Lord God of Hosts." He told his readers that "many facts and providences ... all around us," might not make their way into *THE BAPTIST.* He was reluctant in assuming the additional post of editor, but felt there was no one else to do it. *THE BAPTIST* had a circulation of 1,600 in its first year.

Howell seized on the truth that a newspaper, prepared and distributed in a timely fashion, would break down barriers of isolation. The people of the churches would respond to news from other places, news that gained identity as reliable and educational. Relating these facts to his readers in an October 1845 issue, he said, "The religious press is a noble engine for the dissemination of truth, and the establishment of proper morals. ...The living voice may arouse generous emotions, may produce high and holy determination, but it soon passes away. ...Not so, however, with the printed page, it lives and talks to present and future generations."

Knowing about other denominations, he saw that without bishops and other such leaders, Baptists would come to respect the voice of *THE BAPTIST.* The persuasive words of the paper could affect the readers and help mold the denomination. And he accepted that responsibility.

The paper was to be published monthly, and a subscription cost "one dollar a year, paid in advance." Howell knew the importance of the printed page in shaping thought among Baptist churches and developing spiritual fellowship. He also believed in the axiom used by the paper during its early years, "A Baptist knows why he is a Baptist."

The pastor/editor was known as a leader in other facets of Baptist life. He helped organize societies for education and ministerial improvement, Bible publication and distribution, and Sunday School work. He led in organizing the Baptist General Association of Tennessee and Alabama (1842), to replace an earlier convention that had a short life. Howell also saw the need for a theological seminary and promoted the idea at the 1849 Southern Baptist Convention in Nashville. His dream became reality in 1859 with the birth of the Southern Baptist Theological Seminary — first in Greenville, South Carolina, and then in Louisville, Kentucky.

Howell eventually championed the formation of the Southern Baptist Convention, and he served as the second president, and later

THE BAPTIST.

"And this gospel of the kingdom shall be preached in all the world, for a witness unto all nations."

Published Monthly.   **R. B. C. Howell, Editor,**   One Dollar a Year, paid in advance.

VOL. I.   NASHVILLE, TENNESSEE....JANUARY, 1835.   NO. I.

EDITORIAL.

OUR PAPER.

The January number of the Baptist was issued in the form proposed in our prospectus. We have not learned what our friends thought of it, but for ourselves, we were not pleased with its appearance. We had several objections, the principal one, however, was the stinted size of the margin, which was entirely too small to allow of binding. On consultation, we resolved to change the form, and determined, in order to make our first volume uniform, to reprint, in its present shape, the January number, which will be sent, immediately, to all our subscribers. The additional expense of this measure will not be inconsiderable, and will make it more necessary, and probably, more agreeable, fo our patrons to be prompt in their remittances. Be that as it may, we conceived our pledge to the public that ours shall be equal, in every respect, to any similar work in the western country, required the sacrifice.

We have in our present form, sixteen, instead of thirty-two pages, but they are double their former size. And the blank spaces necessary in the other, being occupied in this, enables us to insert a larger amount of matter, and, at the same time, secure an ample margin. We think the change was every way desirable, and will add materially to the value of our work, especially as it is designed, for preservation, as a permanent record of passing events. We anticipate with confidence the entire approbation, in this respect, of all our readers

The first number of THE BAPTIST, we have, at length, laid before our readers. We confess that we do not, without many fears, and misgivings, enter the Editorial field. The peculiarly disordered state of the Church,

throughout a large portion of this commonwealth, and many other parts of the great valley of the west, growing, as we believe, out of the prevalence of intestine dissensions, the conflict of opinion, on doctrinal, as well as practical religion, and the operation of, perhaps, many other causes equally disturbing, and deleterious, will, we apprehend, render the task of conducting a religious periodical. at the present crisis, extremely arduous. Under the most favorable circumstances, the skill we might bring to the work, would be sufficiently limited. Add inexperienced, as we are, in editorial tactics, and perhaps, in other respects, not so well calculated as many others of our brethren, to sit upon the whirlwind and manage the storm, which now rages in the moral world, we tremble lest we should not be able to accomplish all the good which it is desirable the Baptist should effect. Could the services of any faithful, and competent brother have been obtained, to conduct the work, most gladly should we have remained silent, and thus have avoided a responsibility which we have assumed with so much reluctance. The Pastorship of the Church, and congregation, in this City, was, of itself, enough to occupy all our powers, and fill up every moment of our time, and we should have rejoiced could we have been left free to devote to it our undivided attention. To assume an additional office, and especially one so difficult, and important, we did, by no means desire. But having, under a sense of solemn duty to God, and the church, whose servant we are, consented to do so, our best exertions shall not be wanting to make this paper an agreeable, and edifying visitor in the families, and by the fireside of our beloved brethren and friends.

The field before us is, indeed large, and white unto the harvest. For wisdom, and strength to cast in the sickle and reap, our confidence is in the Lord God of Hosts. Cheered by his countenance and blessing, and governed by the directions of his Holy Spirit,

we shall not, we trust, labor in vain. As to pecuniary advantage, we derive none. We labor without money, and without price. The only reward to which we look, is the hope that through these means, by the blessing of the Lord, we may aid in quieting the jarring elements of discord, and bind to the cross of Jesus the hearts and affections of a larger number of immortal spirits. We are aware that many faithful, pious and talented laborers are already engaged in the same work with ourselves, and the necessity of our publication may, therefore, be questioned. Let it, however, be kept in mind, that all those laborers are at a distance from us. The interest which is felt in a paper conducted in the midst of our own community, is not attached to the works to which we allude. They are not, consequently, patronised to any desirable extent. Not, by any means, because they are not worthy of patronage, but because they cannot, in the nature of things, possess and embody the local information required. Many facts and providences, rich in mercy and constantly occuring around us, and which otherwise would never find a record, will make their way into the Baptist, and will readily and immediately interest all those in whose neighborhood they have transpired. Thus many would be induced to read, who would not otherwise receive a religious paper of any kind. The boundary of their vision enlarged, the children of God will see more of the goodness of his grace; they will have occasion to observe more of the wants of his church, and of the world; and will consequently feel a deeper anxiety for the salvation of sinners. Many, thousands, by these means, perhaps, will find cause for gratitude, and prayer, and effort, who might, under other circumstances, have continued to slumber on, undisturbed. These and similar considerations encourage us to enter upon our work; and the more cheerfully, in the hope that, by the blessing o heaven upon this instrumentality, our Zion

The first issue — January 1835

was elected for two four-year terms. When he was elected in 1859 despite long and heated opposition by J.R. Graves, he immediately resigned to save the convention from bitter debate. Graves, who was to become the second editor of *THE BAPTIST*, opposed Howell for years thereafter. The two had doctrinal differences — Graves promoted Landmarkism, which Howell vigorously opposed. Graves had served as assistant editor of *THE BAPTIST*. Howell made efforts to halt the dissension.

He gave the paper to the Baptist General Association of Tennessee and North Alabama in 1846, but continued as editor. The Association named J.R. Graves as associate editor. Graves became editor in 1848 when Howell moved to Richmond, Virginia, to pastor a church there. In his editor's role, Graves emphasized the supremacy of the local church, and challenged the influence of national cooperative Baptist organizations.

Graves' stance led to the birth of the Landmarkism movement and he became the leader. Howell returned to the pastorate of First Church, Nashville, in 1857. A bitter Howell-Graves controversy ensued, and it dominated the Southern Baptist denomination for decades.

As an editor and Baptist leader, Howell and later editors dealt with name changes, consolidation with other papers, lack of sufficient funding, competition with other papers, mail service, vitriolic letter writers, and changes in journalism.

Howell was a distinguished leader, pastor, editor, and wrote several books on church doctrines. He wrote a history of Nashville's First Baptist Church, 1820-63, while imprisoned by the Federal Government in 1862 for refusing to take an oath of allegiance to the government.

Another Baptist explains that he was the right man in the right place at the right time. Author Joe W. Burton, in his book, *Road to Augusta,* (Broadman Press, Nashville, 1976), writes, "One other thing Howell knew for sure in 1834. He knew his own place in the current movement to bring the Southwest into the kingdom of his Christ. There was no doubt at all in his own mind. He came as a man fully committed to a leadership role. Everything he did betokened this personal knowledge of the leadership position."

And the little town of Nashville was the natural gateway. Water transportation was the principal method of moving people and commerce. Hundreds of riverboats visited the Nashville docks on the Cumberland River — plowing the rivers north, south, and west. The route west went to St. Louis. *THE BAPTIST* would travel west — delivering Baptist news and information, Howell's dream was becoming reality.

From its beginning in 1835, Howell made his paper a strong advocate for cooperative work among Baptist churches. The paper began to solve problems caused by lack of information. It became the method for informing churches about the life and work of Baptists. A few limited circular newsletters in the past could not do the work of a newspaper. Now, *THE BAPTIST* could make it possible for hundreds of Baptists to be better informed by delivering news from far away, connecting its readers with Baptists from other states. Two well-liked features were discussions of doctrinal issues and letters from readers who now had a way to express their opinions. Though lengthy and most often theological in form, editorials were also popular.

Let's look at one of the first "family" fusses witnessed by Howell. The first Tennessee Baptist Convention was formed in 1833, only two years before he began publishing his paper. However, many Baptists disagreed with the action. Missions was at the epicenter of arguments, which dampened the cooperative spirit throughout the 1830s. In September 1838, Howell wrote, "Scarcely was the Convention organized when it was assailed from various quarters, with the intensest zeal and perseverance! The Convention, its friends, and its purposes, were discussed, and condemned in their private circles, and denounced, caricatured, and defamed in nearly every sermon they preached. At the head of the opposition were many persons in the three divisions of the state, both ministers, and laymen of no mean influence."

The Convention was dissolved in 1842, to be followed by the formation of the Baptist General Association of Tennessee. Howell served both as president/moderator for fourteen years, 1835-48. (Other changes were made later, with organizing and reorganizing, and name changing, until the present day Convention was formed in 1874.)

Lack of widespread support was detrimental to anything that resembled control over the local church. And weak means of communication abetted fears of control. When the convention was first formed, there was no Baptist paper. Travel was difficult, harsh. Distances were great and a statewide network of highways did not exist. Frontier preachers were suspicious of "outsiders" such as Howell and other leaders. But Howell's paper, as it gained confidence, helped readers make decisions. Many leaders and readers gradually began to respect the paper. He was a strong advocate of the temperance reform movement and used the pages of *THE BAPTIST* to support his belief.

On another social issue that was tearing apart the nation, Howell did not want states to secede from the Union, and did not oppose slavery. In an 1845 editorial, he wrote that he believed that God established slavery, and he saw that it was not possible to convince Northerners that slavery was not a sin. He believed slavery would cease eventually because of economics.

Though he is well known for founding and editing the paper, Howell was a prolific writer and note-taker apart from the published pages. Among some of his Pastor's Book notes, he wrote that he had preached, "about 9,308 sermons, married 540 couples, and conducted about 4,650 funerals."

Now, some Howell quotes:

The need for theological education — Theological seminaries properly understood and well conducted, are among the most useful institutions that can be formed. They are not designed to fabricate ministers, correct a useless privileged order, or to supply the want of piety and talents; but to foster, and to assist and strengthen those natural and spiritual endowments which, together with a desire to devote themselves to the work, they are required to possess in a good degree, before they can be admitted to enjoy the benefits of such an institution.

Divisions in other denominations (1845) — The most distinguished Baptists of the South have acted on the principle, that whatever divisions might occur among other sects, none among their own should be produced by them ... we have looked to so-called moderate men of the North to protect us, but we have looked in vain. There is a point, beyond which, to yield to outrage is irreligious; and that point we have now reached. Are our Northern brethren asleep? Or do they prefer the fellowship of those disturbers of the peace, to that of the entire South? They can no longer enjoy both!

Status of the church in Tennessee (early edition) — The progress of every portion of the Church in this State is backward. The stand of religion is low. Restlessness and discontent are prominent. The dark picture is relieved only by two or three instances of revival in Eastern and Western districts and in some two or three churches in middle Tennessee.

The need for unity — Conquering armies are formed of individuals acting in concert. This agreement, this union, this concert is a missionary association. ...Why are brethren grieved for our engaging in missionary effort? This effort is not unorthodox in doctrine. It is not immoral. Why then do anti-effort brethren talk of withdrawing from us? We ask no one to do what he is not convinced is according to the will of God. We interfere with no church or association regulation. Will they exclude our brethren because they feel it their duty to labor for the spread of the gospel and the salvation of souls?

R. B. C. Howell, Later Years

Joe Burton said Howell was elected to office in every Baptist body of which he was ever a member, and to every level of official responsibility. He summarized Howell's contributions to the early years of the Southern Baptist Convention, "... the superlative of local church independence and autonomy, the absolute corollary of limited denominational controls, full commitment in time and energy to the ministry, full support by churches of a full-time ministry, specialized training for theological and pastoral ministry, development of a central seminary, the ministry as partnership of pastor and congregation, full and free communication with the people through popular media, and the presidency of the Southern Baptist Convention is secondary to larger kingdom concerns, not to be sought as a political goal or personal treasure."

Rufus Spain wrote in the Tennessee Historical Society Quarterly (1955) that Howell played a major role in the development of the Baptist denomination after 1835. He said, "He led a disunited and retarded frontier denomination in the acceptance of a unified and progressive program ... of denominational unity when these were unpopular in the West."

Burton had persuasive insight on the effect of the Civil War on Howell's life. Referring to Howell's imprisonment, he said, "… he would neither admit any instance of disloyalty as would be implied in voicing the prescribed oath of allegiance nor bow abjectly in a plea for release to the one he called a tyrant [Andrew Johnson, military governor in Nashville]." The prison experience caused Howell to compare the Federal government with churches. In notes written while in prison, Howell said the two are alike especially in voluntary union of the states and union of the churches in associations. However, he believed compelling the unions would destroy each, and the use of coercion to force continuing union would be damaging.

Robert Boyte Crawford Howell was an impressive leader among Baptists, not only with Tennessee and the South, but in his leadership with the Southern Baptist Convention. He had strong and devoted beliefs in missions, education, and doctrine. He was a man with a mission — and Tennessee Baptists in particular are indebted to him for his dedication and his impact for Christ.

The first two editors had opposing views often during their careers as editors and pastors. At times the differences between R.B.C. Howell and J.R. Graves became loud and uncompromising. Sometimes their arguments grew angry, and appeared in print. During some of these "battles" others joined the fray. In particular they disagreed on publishing efforts. W. Fred Kendall writes in his *A History of the Tennessee Baptist Convention,* about one such debate:

"Attacks by Graves, Pendleton, and Dayton [collaborators and friends of Graves] were made on Howell in almost every issue of the *Tennessee Baptist.* Howell never answered these attacks and never entered into debate with the three men, according to records. Revival broke out in First Baptist Church (Nashville) in April 1858, with a spirit of prayer. The results were seventy people baptized, twenty heads of their families, and ninety-six additions to the church, not counting the colored people, of which there were twenty-six.

"Through this time, Howell made every effort to change J.R. Graves and to induce him to cease his attacks. Mutual friends were selected to arrange a meeting. Howell proposed to do anything that truth and honor would justify. Graves refused any measure of relief, and each day he became more violent and abusive. Each week he published attacks of the severest kind which he had selected from

his correspondence and those he had written with his own hand."
(When Graves became editor, he initiated a name change to
Tennessee Baptist.)

This particular argument, though vitriolic and intense, developed
when First Baptist Church, Nashville, attempted to oust Graves
from its members. Eventually the vote was against Graves. However
attacks continued. Since Graves controlled the *Tennessee Baptist*,
the church began its own paper, the *Baptist Standard*, edited by L.B
Woolfolk, a supporter of the church and Howell. The paper was
valuable in getting both sides of the issue to the *Standard* readers.
The arguments became less vitriolic and eventually ceased as letter
writers to the *Standard* began to say, enough.

Witnesses said Graves became a gentler, more forgiving man in
his last days. But it was too late for Howell to know; his latter years
were spent away from Baptist newspapers and family strife. Though
he wasn't reconciled with his former comrade, Howell left a legacy
of foresight, patience, and a stubborn will to invade the wilderness
of souls with the Good News of Jesus Christ.

Bits of Biography, R.B.C. Howell — Native of Wayne County,
North Carolina, March 10, 1801; educated at Columbian
College, Washington, D.C., and Georgetown College, Kentucky;
knew Hebrew, Latin, Greek; Began preaching 1825, ordained in
Cumberland Baptist Church, Norfolk, Virginia, in 1827 where was
called; moved to Nashville, Tennessee, 1834, to become pastor of
First Baptist Church; founded *THE BAPTIST* newspaper 1835, and
was connected to the paper until 1848 when James R. Graves
became sole editor; called to Second Baptist Church, Richmond,
Virginia, 1850, serving until 1857 when he was recalled to Nashville;
married Mary Ann Morton Toy; was instrumental in laying the foundation for the Southern Baptist Convention and was vice president
in its early years, and again after serving as president for several
years, president of the Tennessee State Baptist Convention and of
the Western Baptist Convention, president of the Bible Board,
Foreign Mission Board, and Southern Baptist Publication Society;
author of *The Deaconship*, 1846, and other books. Died April 5,
1868.

CHAPTER TWO

Growth and Dissension
James Robinson Graves
1848-89

The Tennessee scene changes and new players enter. The ongoing drama draws the attention of the audience. Wait, the leading characters are still in place. Their roles change only as tensions of the drama increase.

Seldom have key actors and interlopers struggled so mightily on stage, defending their ideas and doctrines before a live audience. Seldom has a star shone so brightly and for so long.

Now, that star, the second editor of *THE BAPTIST* comes on stage, able and ready to take his place as featured player. James R. Graves appears. He came to Nashville in 1845 as a bit player on the denominational stage. He opened the Vine Street Classical and Mathematical Academy and joined First Baptist Church. Soon thereafter he became pastor of Central Baptist Church — and was asked by R.B.C. Howell to join him at *THE BAPTIST* as assistant editor.

Graves became the paper's editor in 1848 when Howell resigned temporarily. He later became owner. He retired in 1889, but continued as a contributing editor until 1893. The new leader had become a scholar and editor with vigor. He soon was recognized as a gifted and dominant speaker, preacher, and Baptist leader.

He was only twenty-six when he became Howell's assistant at *THE BAPTIST*. No one dreamed that the argumentative teacher from Vermont would serve as editor of *THE BAPTIST* for forty-one years, though the paper later had other names. His role on the stage of Tennessee Baptist life was not over, however. He would be an influence on that stage possibly more than anyone except Howell, who also was known as one of the outstanding leaders in the denomination.

Describing Graves, the man, Walter Shurden said, "He was a pastor, evangelist, editor, author, publisher, denominational leader: he was many things, but most of all he was a controversialist! Possessed with an overdose of charisma and locomotive energy, he drove himself tirelessly." (*Not a Silent People: Controversies That Have Shaped Southern Baptists*, Walter B. Shurden, Broadman Press, Nashville, 1972)

Beginning with Howell and Graves, the first two editors of the first paper, for eighty-five years, editors and publishers owned the paper. For the next eighty-five years the Tennessee Baptist Convention's Executive Board has owned it.

He differed with Howell on some doctrinal issues, and agreed on others. They often swapped accusations and angry letters. Howell, perhaps sensed their arguments were harmful to Tennessee Baptists, and Southern Baptists. Strong-willed and steeped in conservative biblical doctrine, both men were willing to fight for their beliefs. Howell later may have regretted choosing Graves to be his associate in producing *THE BAPTIST*.

Graves varied the paper's name, using *THE BAPTIST* and *Tennessee Baptist* from time to time. His years as editor were colored by denominational controversy, personal attacks, and pointed and confrontational editorials. He took on editors and papers of other denominations fearlessly. Because of his adherence to Landmarkism, he especially criticized the doctrines and policies of Methodists.

Perhaps the most extreme example was a bold thrust at Methodists. Graves developed a series of open letters to Bishop Sole, a Methodist leader, into a book, *The Great Iron Wheel*, which he published. Even so, he became known as a powerful editor and businessman, operating publishing houses.

Graves is best known for his connection with Landmarkism. This movement dominated Baptist life for several decades. We will not attempt to explore Landmarkism thoroughly in this brief history. A short explanation is appropriate.

Walter Shurden, in a Baptist Heritage pamphlet (see Prologue for title of his book on the same subject), calls the movement one of several serious crises in Southern Baptist life. He says, "The movement [Landmarkism] began among Southern Baptists in the early 1850s and insisted that Baptist churches are the only true churches. Therefore, Baptist churches must abide by the old landmarks. The name came from two Old Testament passages: 'Remove not the ancient landmark, which thy fathers have set.' (Proverbs 22:28), and 'Some remove the landmarks... .' " (Job 24:2)

Graves and his followers applied the word to what they believed to be endangered Baptist distinctives.

Shurden says, "A 'landmark' was, therefore, an ancient Baptist principle. The problem was that certain 'landmarks' were not as ancient as Landmarkers suggested."

Graves himself was the founder and "high priest" of Landmarkism, says Shurden, and he led the movement from its beginning in 1851, and aimed to make its theology dominant among Southern Baptists. Using the paper and other publications, he spread Landmarkism among Baptists across the South and Southwest. Some Baptist historians say during the nineteenth century, Graves may have influenced Baptist life more than any other person.

According to the *Encyclopedia of Southern Baptists*, "As an agitator and controversialist of the first magnitude, he (Graves) kept his denomination in almost continual and often bitter controversy for about thirty years. He also engaged in frequent and prolonged debates and controversies with outstanding representatives of other denominations. Being magnetic and dynamic, he won the enthusiastic and loyal support of thousands, but being acrimonious in his disputations and attacks, he made many determined enemies."

During the period 1858-59, Graves led a strong effort to relieve the Foreign Mission Board (Southern Baptist, and now International Mission Board) of its power "to examine, choose, support, and direct it missionaries." He claimed those were the rights of churches and associations. His proposal was defeated at Richmond, Virginia, in 1859, during a daylong session during which Graves spoke for several hours.

In the 1850s Graves strongly challenged the Southern Baptist Publication Society, accusing it of publishing materials for the churches that had doctrinal deviations, and thus failed to meet the people's needs. Using his paper, a personal tract society, and his publishing firm, he actively competed with the publication society.

It was his intention to provide the major Baptist publication out-
let in the South. Because of heavy printing costs and the development and outcome of the Civil War, all of his several efforts at publication failed, as did some of others.

Graves was noted also as a powerful
speaker. T.T. Eaton, in a *Western Recorder*
(Kentucky) editorial, wrote when Graves
died, "We have seen him hold a congregation packed uncomfortably, for three
hours and a half without any sign of
weariness on their part. This was not
done once or twice, but scores of times."

That he was editor of Tennessee
Baptists' newspaper for forty-one years is
testimony to his strength, determination,
courage, and ability. Though he could be

James Robinson Graves

a menacing adversary, during his latter years as editor his attitude
was softer. *The Encyclopedia of Southern Baptists* says, "... the year
his publication society failed (1877), reveals that the man of thunder
and conflict had subsided and a man of gentler and sweeter spirit
was developing. He gave much less attention to controversial matters and dealt much more gently with those who did not agree with
him. ... It is this Graves his friends and admirers, and their descen-
dants, largely remember."

An item appearing in several issues of *THE BAPTIST* indicates
Graves' readiness to point out bad characters among pastors. From
the June 3, 1882 issue, we read under the heading "The Detective."

Graves wrote. "Under this head we shall insert and keep standing
for the benefit of the denomination, the names of every imposter
and excluded Baptist preacher known to us, as reference to prove his
guilt.

"T.M. Hazlewood — reference, Ben McBryan, church clerk,
Asheville Association.

"Edward Harris — reference, J.W. Wann, church clerk, Carrollton
Church, Arkansas.

"Elder Robert Tomlin — reference, Elder A.J. Peddy, Hemphill,
Texas.

"T.C.M. Gilland — reference, W.B. Crumpton, Shield's Mill,
Alabama.

"Rev. A.G. Jones, alias Geo. Jones — reference, *Biblical Recorder*, Raleigh, North Carolina."

These names were repeated June 12, June 24, and July 1. There was no notice whether these "imposters" were arrested or cleared. But Graves, though his proof of guilt was not specified, pointed out the "errors."

Readers of Graves' publications, including *THE BAPTIST* (sometimes called *Tennessee Baptist*), were aware usually of his motives, his targets. He was outspoken and did not mince words. He was editor, owner, and sometimes publisher. His co-owners agreed with his theology, and therefore, like most editors of that era, editorials and essays could be written with a fearless style.

In 1849, one of his early issues, he told his readers some of his plans. Often it was difficult to determine which pages contained editorials, since much of the material was loaded with opinion. This seemed to be the norm in many of the early Baptist newspapers.

On what seems to be an editorial page in the 1849 issue, he wrote a special message for readers: "The *Tennessee Baptist* for 1850! Especially commended to the notice of every Baptist, friendly to the uncompromising advocacy of Baptist principles, and opposed to error: who love the pure Republican principles of the gospel and primitive Christianity, and are opposed to despotic hierarchies and human traditions."

Graves was not reluctant to praise his own efforts, even though his editorials and opinion pieces often were inflammatory.

He continued his 1849 message by reminding his audience that his paper "… is the oldest and cheapest paper in the whole South, or South West! It has already attained the largest subscription list of any Baptist paper in the whole South.… This is owing to its open and undaunted advocacy of Baptist principles, and its uncompromising opposition to error, human traditions, and ecclesiastical usurpation and despotism."

Graves warned readers that a series of special articles would be discussed in 1850s issues, the first being "The claims of existing churches examined by the model churches in the New Testament."

When editors of other papers responded to his caustic editorials, he replied to them, or allowed a like-minded writer to reply.

He outlined some policies for the paper. Here is an example: "The courts have decided that refusing to take a newspaper or periodical from the office, or removing and leaving it uncalled for, until all arrearages are paid, is prima facie evidence of intentional fraud."

In an article called "Family Adviser," for housewives, readers were given directions for making water cold in summer.

Now for some examples of Graves' editorials and opinion articles:

On religious intolerance — There is nothing to the mind of a true American more hateful than the spirit of religious intolerance.

Our next volume — One more paper will close the present volume (August 23,1849 issue). Many are doubtless deciding whether they will continue subscribers another year. The few weeks about to close of a year are full of anxiety to the editor of a public journal.... Let those who discontinue, remember to pay up all arrearages. ... This is the law of all newspapers.

From his book, *Old Landmarkism: What Is It?* — In 1846 I took charge of the *Tennessee Baptist*, and soon commenced agitating the question of the validity of alien immersion, and the propriety of Baptists recognizing, by any act, ecclesiastical or ministerial, Pedobaptist Societies or preachers as churches and ministers of Christ. [This statement of exclusivism is the essence of Landmarkism. — Editor's note]

Thoughts on giving — Whatever views Christians may entertain in regard the Millennium, it is unquestionably their duty to see that the gospel is preached in all the world, to every creature. Those who believe that Christ will reign personally on earth during the millennial era should be diligently engaged in preparing for His coming. Let them instrumentally accomplish the salvation of as many sinners as possible. ... What I mean to say is, that a belief in the personal reign of Christ during the Millennium, and in the nearness of the day of his coming, cannot legitimately extinguish missionary zeal, but must kindle it into a flame, and induce a liberal consecration of money to the cause of missions.

Answering a question from reader A. Swindal, 1860 — The question: Were the twelve apostles and seventy disciples converted previous to the day of Pentecost, and if so, at what time and place? Graves' answer: John unquestionably baptized them, and they brought forth fruits meet for repentance, or renewed hearts and faith in Christ, before he baptized them.

On hard times in war, December, 1861 — It would be difficult to find any family, or an individual, in these Confederate States suffering for want of the substantial comforts of life. Many find it necessary to forego the luxuries and unrestrained indulgence of their tastes and fancies to which they have been accustomed. And therefore is, in most parts of the country, a great scarcity of money. Even those, however, who make the greatest outcry about the "hard times," appear to be comfortably clad, and their daily tables are spread with an abundance of wholesome and palatable food. ... We do not deny that our people are called to endure many privations, and to make great sacrifices beyond what has ever before fallen to their lot. ... It is a sin and a shame to indulge in whining complaints and doleful lamentations. We might fill columns with an exposition of its meanness and wickedness. ... Let us beware of murmuring against Divine Providence. When the Lord led His ancient people from a land of bondage and tyranny to freedom and independence, He conducted them through a wilderness.... .

News items from 1862 — From Richmond, Virginia: Congress passed, and the President has approved, an act authorizing the President to enlist for the war such seamen, not exceeding two thousand, as the exigencies of the naval service for the defence of the sea-coast, rivers, and harbours, may render necessary. An act was also passed admitting Kentucky as a member of the Confederate States, on an equal footing with other States of the Confederacy.

Gen. Halleck (Federal) issued a savage proclamation on the sixth. He will shoot rebels captured as spies. Many Unionists from South Western Missouri are in St. Louis in a deplorable condition, they say caused by Price's army. *The Democrat* recommends that they be quartered with rebel families in St. Louis.

Editorial note, 1876 — The outlook of the present is sufficient to fill us all with the gravest apprehensions for the long continuance of natural peace and safety. There are two governors in the State of South Carolina, and the prospect is that there will be two presidents inaugurated the fourth of next March, unless the supreme crisis is precipitated at the counting of the electoral votes.

James R. Graves had the tenacity and spiritual depth to lead the Baptist newspaper during some bright and growing years. He joined R.B.C. Howell in the legendary role of editing a paper that, despite some years of controversy, was the first and finest in Tennessee

Baptist life. It was known to be an enthusiastic supporter of Tennessee Baptist churches, and purveyor of news events from around the world. The "old landmarker" was not afraid to address, on the pages of *THE BAPTIST* (and *Tennessee Baptist*), any problem and to avidly promote any friendly belief or doctrine. From the May 2, 1935, Centennial issue of the *B&R*, it was noted that, "J.R. Graves was a Baptist without apology. It has been freely said that in an unusually marked degree he helped Baptists to find and to know themselves, and that Baptist orthodoxy throughout the South still shows his impress."

Bits of Biography, James R. Graves — Born in Chester, Vermont, April 10, 1820; converted and joined North Springfield Baptist Church, Vermont; at age nineteen elected principal of an academy in Kingsville, Ohio; moved to Nicholasville, Kentucky as head of Clear Creek Academy; spent four years studying to become a pastor; during these studies he became a Baptist scholar, ordained at age twenty-four; moved to Nashville in 1845, opened Vine Street Classical and Mathematical Academy; called in 1846 to work with R.B.C. Howell at *THE BAPTIST*, became editor in 1848, served until 1889; authored many books, and was a noted speaker. Died June 26, 1893.

CHAPTER THREE

Reaching Beyond Borders
Edgar E. Folk
1889-1917

Edgar E. Folk, third editor of the *Baptist and Reflector*, has the distinction of being a Tennessee native, the first native-born editor. History does not record how he felt about following the two giants, R.B.C. Howell and J.R. Graves. But we do know that his loyalty to Christ Jesus gave him the courage to follow their best motives — supplying weekly information and inspiration to enable the churches to work together.

Folk also possessed interest in journalism as did Howell and Graves. He had observed their use of the printed page to supply needed information to the thousands of Tennessee Baptists, and realized the urgency of continuity. In the 125th anniversary edition of the *Baptist and Reflector,* letters of congratulation from the stronger papers were used. Floyd Looney, editor of the *California Southern Baptist* in 1959, wrote that E.E. Folk's son was his journalism professor.

Here's what Looney wrote, after expressing appreciation for *B&R* editors John D. Freeman, O.W. Taylor, and Richard N. Owen: "I also with no little pride trace my professional ancestry back to the *Baptist and Reflector*. Dr. E.E. Folk, now a professor at Wake Forest College in North Carolina, was my journalism teacher when I was a student at Oklahoma Baptist University more than a quarter of a century ago. He is a gifted and scholarly son of a former editor of the *Baptist and Reflector*." Is it possible that Looney's journalism professor learned something of his vocation from his "journalistic father?"

He is remembered also for bringing together editors from all the Southern Baptist state papers. Folk, in a stroke of marvelous accord and peacemaking, was the founding father of Southern Baptist Press Association (now called Association of Southern Baptist State Papers) in 1895. He sensed that editors needed to have fellowship, to review their roles, and to work together in supporting the state conventions. He championed freedom of the press, but also recognized that this freedom carries great responsibility as an equal partner.

The organization meets twice annually, and celebrated its centennial in 1995 by publishing its own history — *Contending for the Right to Know*, by C. William Junker. At the meetings, editors have shared ideas and discussed problems such as the postal system and its costs, financial stability, printing procedures and policies, page design, and editorial topics.

Folk was one of the editors who reported to his readers news after attending the meetings. Occasionally he listed the names (with newspaper titles) of those who attended. In the early years, the sessions were social affairs as well. Readers could thus "get acquainted" with editors and papers of other state conventions.

Though the early years of state papers were dominated by controversy and quarreling, Folk believed in "trusting God and telling the people." The most likely purpose for organizing was stated by Folk: "We may simply say it will, we believe, tend to promote a greater spirit of fraternity among the editors and other representatives of our Southern Baptist papers, and so will be in the direction of building up our common Zion. We may also, I think, be of much benefit to one another along business lines." The group was organized in Atlanta, November 28, 1895. The ASBP still meets regularly.

Folk was elected secretary at the first meeting, and was re-elected six terms. He was president of SBPA in 1903, and later *B&R* editors also served as president — John D. Freeman (4), O.W. Taylor (2), Richard Owen, Alvin Shackleford, Wm. Fletcher Allen, and the current editor, Lonnie Wilkey.

Folk also has the second longest tenure at the paper's helm. His twenty-eight years is next to Graves' forty-one.

He had been a pastor in Murfreesboro, Tennessee, as well as churches in Kentucky and Georgia before moving to the editorship of the *American Baptist Reflector* in Chattanooga, Tennessee, in 1889.

Here is where the trail gets somewhat complicated. Several changes were made among leaders and owners of a handful of Baptist papers — and the *Baptist and Reflector* emerged unchallenged as the official newsjournal. Pity the neophyte historian in trying to follow the somewhat tangled path of Baptist newspapers in Tennessee.

The late Richard N. Owen, former editor 1950-68, explained the changes in the July 18, 1974, special edition of the paper:

"*THE BAPTIST* (again) became *Tennessee Baptist,* September 9, 1882, then five years later reverted to the shorter name following merger with *The Baptist Gleaner* of Fulton, Kentucky, owned and edited by J.B. Moody of Paducah. He became co-owner with J.R. Graves in 1887. Graves' son-in-law, O.L. Hailey, bought Moody's interest, was given Graves' interest, and became editor before *THE BAPTIST* merged with *American Baptist Reflector* of Chattanooga in August 1889.

"E.E. Folk was editor of *American Baptist Reflector.* The combined papers became *Baptist and Reflector* and moved publication to Nashville in 1889.

"It is well to note that Morristown, Tennessee, was home for the *Reflector* where it began by O.C. Pope. The paper was published in Nashville from 1878 to 1882 when it merged with *The Baptist Sun* of Rome, Georgia, and began publication in Chattanooga. Inn 1885 it was bought by A.W. McGaha and R.J. Willingham who was later head of the Foreign Mission Board, SBC. From these two owners, *American Baptist Reflector's* ownership passed to Folk."

Edgar E. Folk, Early Years

The first issue of the *Baptist Reflector* published and edited by Pope has some noteworthy information. As the hourglass was running out, names and owners of Baptist papers were dwindling to a short list. Pope, a Tennessee Baptist leader, was one of many whom supported the idea for a reputable paper that would serve all Tennessee Baptists — from east to west, north to south.

Whether Folk was cognizant of this, we do not know. But Pope, aided by four "corresponding editors" began publishing this new paper on November 25, 1875. It was a noble effort. As Albert Wardin points out in his *Tennessee Baptists, a Comprehensive History, 1779-1999,* this was the third attempt to establish a Baptist paper in Nashville after the Civil War. And the new paper was one of the strongest competitors for *THE BAPTIST.* Pope soon hired William Huff in Middle Tennessee as associate editor. He wanted it to become the Baptist paper for Tennessee. This is when Pope sold to W.D. Mayfield who moved it to Nashville.

On the editorial page of that first issue of *The Baptist Reflector,* Pope wrote about the recent Tennessee Baptist Convention meeting that he had attended, and had actively participated. In it he reminded readers of the need for a viable Baptist newspaper for the entire state.

Remember that the latter years of the 1800s were years of building leadership, winnowing down the many Baptist papers of Tennessee. State papers were being developed elsewhere. Editors of spiritual strength, courage, and leadership were necessary if strong papers were to survive as voices of the people and messengers of news. They would make the difference in survival.

Also, the developing papers had to possess soundness of character, solid ownership, the best locations, and an honest name.

So it was during these perilous years that E.E. Folk came on the scene as editor of the surviving *Baptist and Reflector.* The paper proved to be the strong voice for Tennessee Baptists. These were years of tumult and discord. The Civil War was still on the minds of most people of the South. Poverty was the lifestyle for many. Government was not the supplier of good will and togetherness. In fact, there was an aura of distrust across the South. But with one reliable Baptist paper, edited with a kinder, less abrasive style of leadership, Baptists could move forward.

The idea of a merger was not new. As early as 1888, Folk had suggested a merger of the two prominent papers. Graves scoffed at the proposal, and wrote a sound denunciation in a December 23 editorial in *THE BAPTIST.*

He wrote, "Well, if Tennessee Baptists, Middle or East, prefer the *Reflector* to the 'old banner' that has been true to their interests for the past thirty years, they can do so: but it is time for friends of the old banner to know what is sought to be done — supplant it in its own field; and unless they are willing to see it done, to go to work at once — earnest to prevent it."

The following year, a *BAPTIST* editorial attacked again: "The oldest and best established papers are barely holding up, and some of them sinking money weekly; and yet the mania for starting new papers was never at a higher pitch. … It is firmly believed that there is money in it, while generations of editors and publishers have testified and demonstrated by failure, that very few have ever made a religious paper pay its way. The brethren are not satisfied with one paper for a State, but must have two, and some, like Missouri and Tennessee, three to a State. Well, it is a free country."

Wardin notes that Tennessee Baptists were fortunate "… in their efforts to achieve unity and progress, that such a man as Folk would take Graves' mantle. … Although he admitted that he was not in complete theological accord with editors of *THE BAPTIST*, he was willing to work in harmony for the common cause. The paper under Folk did not deviate from Landmark principles but was not as ideologically strident as *THE BAPTIST* and was much less confrontational with other Baptist editors and other denominations." And, he said, "Folk was a strong promoter of the entire denominational program on both the state and national levels."

The first two editors had fought the battles with other denominations and with other Baptists about their views of Baptist distinctives. The battlegrounds were beginning to clear. It was said by one speaker that, "Baptists are not like anyone else except themselves."

In a concise authentication of Baptists, Frank S. Mead wrote a little book called *The Baptists.* Published first in 1934, and later updated by Broadman Press, it had only fifty-five pages. But the entire book is complimentary. He summed up his definition of Baptists, and how they had shaped history with this last pungent paragraph:

"The world has done its best to stop them. We can trace their history more readily in the bloody footprints of their martyrs than in the ink of their historians. We have tried to shame them by whipping them, and they have made us ashamed of our whipping posts.

"We chained them in jail and discovered that the other end of the chain was fast about our own necks. We let their blood in Boston and the South, only to find the fairest American flowers we know growing from that very soil. Addlepated world! You have tried to stamp them out, and all you got for it was to have them leave their stamp on you!"

No doubt R.B.C. Howell and J.R. Graves, and also Folk would have appreciated such a tribute. He spoke to this subject in an editorial August 27, 1896. He had been editor of the consolidated *Baptist and Reflector* since 1889. Folk wrote:

"With this issue we begin a new volume of the *Baptist and Reflector*. It is the sixtieth volume of *THE BAPTIST*, the twenty-sixth of the *Baptist Reflector*, and the eighth of the *Baptist and Reflector*. It has been seven years since the two papers were consolidated. ... They have been years of doubt and uncertainty, of struggles and trials and much hard work, but at the same time we are glad now to say that they have been years also of hope and joy, of triumph and reward. We have seen the paper grow constantly in the affections of the brethren, judging from the continued expressions which have come from them. ... We have seen it become more and more firmly established from a financial point of view until now, we believe, its future is assured beyond a shadow of doubt."

The editor continually expressed confidence in the paper's value to the churches and individuals:

"At the same time we have seen our Baptist cause prosper in this State as never before. The Baptists of the State have learned to know and to love one another better. They have come closer together, and have joined hands more earnestly for the accomplishment of the Master's work in the State. In missions, in education, and all along the lines there has been a constant advance," he wrote.

He enumerated advances in missions, programs, stewardship, and new work, and noted that nearly all the churches had pastors.

"We believe the future of the Baptists in Tennessee is bright and promising," he wrote. "We do not claim that all of these advancements have been due to the *Baptist and Reflector*, but we believe that we can modestly and truthfully claim that the paper has had some share in the good work, furnishing as it has done the medium of communication for the brethren all over the state, through which they could cheer one another in their respective labors for the Master.

"And if we have been instrumental in the least degree in helping along the glorious work, we shall feel fully repaid for all the trials and toils and sacrifices which we have endured during these years in order to accomplish these results.

"And now let us close ranks ... and march forward to the accomplishments of still grander things for the Master ... and may Christ be our Captain and the Holy Spirit our guide."

In a major editorial of December 27, 1900, E.E. Folk looked at history, and turned toward the future. He noted that, "At the close of the eighteenth century, the world was pretty much the same as it had been for several hundred years, and in many important respects about the same as it had been for several thousand years." He wrote about the many changes, and much progress made in the nineteenth century. He marveled at the many inventions and worldwide growth in many areas. He concluded that his century was one of improvements across the globe. He said, "Along social and moral lines, it has been a century of marvelous advancement. The influence of America made a republic of France, a modified form of monarchy out of England, overthrew the theory of divine rights of Kings, and has abolished despotism in every nation of Europe except Turkey and Russia."

History should be more than a jumble of facts as James L. Sullivan said many years later. When he was president of the Baptist Sunday School Board (LifeWay Christian Resources), he made the comment when asked for his definition of history. In the Prologue of this book, he said history is like a river with tributaries flowing into it, comparing the river to history. From the beginning of the *Baptist and Reflector* until Folk's years as editor, the paper was both a mighty river and a jumble of facts.

The river's route, with its many tributaries, may seem confusing, but the end result gave Tennessee Baptists perhaps the best of all those streams through history — almost like a treasured recipe handed down from generations past.

In another editorial, perhaps as vital as any he wrote, he pointed to several differences among Southern Baptists which had the potential of dividing the Convention. Some of the differences exist even today. He gave evidence of the problems, and suggested a solution for remaining together. Some editors even now may grapple with some of those differences. In the January 5, 1899, editorial titled "Shall Southern Baptists Divide?," he wrote:

"Let us have our principles. Let us hold to them as tenaciously as we please. Let us promulgate them earnestly and try to induce others to adopt them. But let us not make them tests of orthodoxy, within the limits of essential Baptist principles, and drive. Let none attempt to injure others. Let us remember that 'we be brethren.' Let us pursue a live-and-let-live policy. 'With malice toward none, with charity for all,' let us live together and work together, as we have done for fifty years."

The editors used the paper to share Baptist news and items of interest, often written as aids for the churches, but also to inform the readers of events from around the world. Some of the news was not related to Baptist (or Christian) work. There had been changes of names and size and number of pages, changes of ownership, use

Ad from January 1, 1903 issue

of advertisements and artwork, reports from correspondents, letters and responses, competition with other Baptist papers as well as those of other denominations.

Edgar Folk usually had on one or more pages, a feature he called "Personal and Practical." These pages were dedicated to a variety of items by and about churches and individuals, some about travels or global politics. Some examples:

"We received a letter several days ago dated 'Beaver Dam.' The writer requested an early reply, and no doubt is expecting one. He will have to be a little more explicit, however, in his directions before we can succeed in reaching him."

"We have been completely overrun with news articles during the last week or two. These have preference over everything else, and in our last issue we gave them the right of way, and left over some very excellent articles which were already in type. We are glad to receive the news. We should like to ask our correspondents, however, to give us the information about their churches in the briefest space possible. Remember that this is the essence of revivals, and that many others over the State are writing similar articles about the revivals in their own churches."

A news item from August 1896, quotes Dr. J. M. King of New York in a lecture given in Cincinnati: "The redemption of the Republic and the perpetuation of American Christian and political institutions will ultimately come from and depend upon the populations of the States south of the Mason and Dixon line." Folk remarked, "If this prophecy be true, how much depends upon efforts for christianizing those rapidly increasing populations. In view of the large percentage of Southern population that is depending upon Baptist sources and Baptist influences, the Home Mission Board, is a factor in the accomplishment of the great work for the American continent."

Excerpts from an article written by A.J. Holt, TBC corresponding secretary (executive director), concerning financial problem — Contributions to State Missions have been steadily decreasing for about two years. The effort to build up all our missionary work on a solid basis, and to induce systematic contributions in the place of high pressure ones, has been the main cause of this falling off … . The exciting political campaign now prevailing is not only absorbing the attention of the people to the neglect of their religion, but their money is being freely spent, thus cutting short the contributions of many to the cause of Christ. One man, a Baptist, spent $1,500 in his race for office last month, then got himself beaten. His pastor said that this was ten times as much as he had ever given to religious purposes. Still men cry 'hard' times when solicited for contributions for missions.

Personal and practical on lynching, answering another paper's chiding — The *Journal and Messenger* is mistaken if it supposes that we apologize for lynching. The editor of that paper has certainly not read the columns of the *Baptist and Reflector* very closely for some years past if he has got such an impression. No paper in the South has spoken out more frequently or strongly in condemnation of lynching than have we. Nor do we believe that the mere fact of attaching the death penalty to the crime of rape will be sufficient to prevent lynching. ... We suggest to the *Journal and Messenger* that if, instead of devoting so much of its space to lynchings in the South, it should give some attention towards trying to secure an amendment of the laws of his own State, which are an outrage upon civilization and a standing inducement both to rape and lynching, it might accomplish more good, on the principle that the best way to keep the streets of Jerusalem clean was for each one to sweep before his own door."

Like those who preceded him, E.E. Folk editorialized or commented on a variety of subjects. Some are still "hanging around" in the year 2005. Here are editorial excerpts:

Capital punishment — It is announced by a member-elect of the Tennessee legislature to assemble next January, that he will introduce a bill to abolish capital punishment. We do not know how the bill will be received. But we want to say very earnestly that we hope it will not pass. There is a kind of sickly sentimentality nowadays growing out of a morbid humanitarianism which is opposed to the death penalty. ... This proposition to abolish capital punishment is another effort to subordinate the rights of society to those of the individual. ... And it could mean the reign of the mob. For in cases of murder or rape the people would rise up in their wrath and take the life of the criminal anyhow. It would simply be transferring the administration of justice from the courthouse to Judge Lynch's court in the woods.

Caring for retired pastors — Editor Folk urged Tennesseans to remember "the old ministers." To his readers he said, "They have labored long and well. They have borne the heat and burden of the day. They have laid the foundations for our Baptist cause in various localities throughout the State. They have gone oftentimes to out-of-the-way places where Baptist preaching had never been heard. During their active ministry their salary was little enough. ... They have worn themselves out in the work of the Lord. ... Shall they be turned out like an old horse, to get their living as best they can? Would it not be more Christianlike, to say the least, that these old ministers ... should be cared for by those whom they have given their lives?" He also noted that a national census report list the average annual salary for Baptist pastors was $333.

Disaster relief — A terrible flood swept over upper East Tennessee last week, resulting in much destruction to houses and livestock and crops, and in the loss of some fifteen or twenty lives. The damage was estimated at about $2 million. ... We have asked Brother Waller, pastor of the Baptist church of Elizabethton, to give our readers an account of the flood and whether the local Baptists will need assistance in any way. [He also wrote about a severe wind storm over West Tennessee, with great damage, especially at Ripley. Is this an inkling of the current disaster relief work?]

The Confederacy, May 30, 1901 — The Confederate Reunion at Memphis this week is very largely attended. It was expected there would be about 100,000 visitors present. These annual reunions of the heroes of a generation ago are occasions of the deepest interest. They are not intended to imply any disloyalty to the present government of the United States, but are only for the purpose of recalling and preserving the brave deeds and hallowed memories of the long ago. Remnants of a once mighty army, these old heroes are but shadowy reminiscences of a past now fading into distant history.

Early Baptist churches — In a letter to the *Baptist Standard* recently on the subject, "Wales, the cradle of Baptist Principles," Dr. Owen A. Williams said: "There is an authentic record of an organized Baptist church at Olchon in the year 1033, and of a Second Baptist church at Illston in 1640, and of a third at Hengoed in 1650." It will be observed that the first of these churches was organized before 1641.

But Edgar Folk was more than a Baptist editor. He was active as a leader among Tennessee Baptists. He was involved in the fight against alcohol, and led the anti-saloon organization. He served on several Tennessee Baptist Convention committees, and he was a leader in forming the SBC's Baptist Sunday School Board in 1891, and also served as president of the publishing organization's board. When the Board was struggling for survival during its early years, Folk provided space in his office for J. M. Frost, the Board's first secretary (president).

Folk, Murphy Cooper, and perhaps other editors, sacrificed personal assets to keep the paper publishing.

The matter of finances was a continuing problem for the paper. Folk and Cooper, and perhaps others, sacrificed personal assets to keep the paper publishing. In the years before the TBC purchased the *Baptist and Reflector* in 1921, sufficient income seemed to be a constant problem. Occasionally, an editor might mortgage his personal home and use savings to pay for printing and other expenses.

When the centennial issue of the *Baptist and Reflector* was produced in 1935, Editor O.W. Taylor asked readers to contribute memories from past papers and editors. William C. Golden wrote from retirement in Orlando, Florida. Golden had served as Tennessee Baptists' executive secretary 1902-20. (In 1943, Tennessee Baptists' state missions offering was named for Mildred and William Golden, honoring their work in state missions.) Golden wrote, among

Edgar E. Folk, Later Years

other things, about E.E. Folk and the *Baptist and Reflector*. He said of Folk, "Dr. Folk had to go in debt to get the *Baptist and Reflector*, and never was free from debt for the paper. He was my beloved brother. ... Many false stories were circulated about Dr. Folk by political enemies and whiskey drinkers, bootleggers, etc. He was accused of making much money out of the paper, which was untrue. I have known him to borrow money to run the paper over summer months. ... He wore himself out serving his brethren and the Baptist cause. Tennessee Baptists owe him a debt they can never pay in this world."

Bits of Biography, Edgar E. Folk — Third editor of the *Baptist and Reflector,* born in Haywood County, Tennessee, September 6, 1856; graduated with MA from Wake Forest College, North Carolina, 1877, and DD also Wake Forest 1895; graduated from Southern Baptist Theological Seminary, 1888; married Elizabeth Handy, they had five children. He was a pastor in Murfreesboro, Tennessee, and Millersburg, Kentucky; authored several books, including *The Mormon Monster.* Died February 27, 1917.

CHAPTER FOUR

New Owners and Short Tenures

Albert Bond, M.R. Cooper, Hight C. Moore

1917-21

The era of long editorial tenures ended temporarily in 1917. After Edgar Folk's death that year three editors followed, all with short terms — Albert Bond, Murphy R. Cooper, and Hight C. Moore, the latter in a "caretaker" role.

Now the newspaper of Tennessee Baptists faced a new day under different circumstances. There were decisions which would shape the future of the paper. Across the state, in a quarter of a century, other papers were consolidated. Finally a name, just one name, was established. Potential readers would be able to identify their own Baptist newspaper. Tennesseans began to reach out across denominational borders and more pastors were getting theological education.

A most important change for the *Baptist and Reflector* had been a long time in the making. In 1921 the Tennessee Baptist Convention purchased the newspaper. No more would there be editors who own the paper, or share ownership with publishers. No longer would an editor be faced with providing all of the income needed to publish — but income depended largely on subscriptions and advertising Strangely enough, the Convention did not agree to provide funding — not just yet. So one problem had been solved, but the financial monster was still alive.

A new editor had to be named to fill Folk's shoes. In only five years, three will serve as editor. Circumstances provided the scenario for leadership changes. Three editors had nurtured the paper for eighty-two years. Under the guidance of R.B.C. Howell, J.R. Graves, and Folk, the paper was well-established, but had barely survived wars, financial problems, debates and personal attacks, heartaches, and struggles for recognition as reliable and thoroughly Baptist, Southern Baptist. In fact, the paper did not publish some months during the Civil War.

During the years of winnowing papers to only one, there were occasions for acting editors, interim editors, or co-editors. These were short-term, but nonetheless important in the life of the *B&R*. Sources don't agree always in unsettled situations. But if the name was listed in the paper as editor — that may prevent disagreement. So three served briefly in 1917-21.

Months before his death, Folk had seen "the handwriting on the wall." He was optimistic about the success of the paper, but he was a realist also. He had favored private ownership of the paper, even though some papers, including the *Baptist and Reflector*, had "silent" partners for financial support. Competition by the secular press was getting stronger. Publication costs increased. Secular papers had more income from subscriptions, and advertising brought in substantial support for them. Ads in secular publications had broader guidelines. In his *Tennessee Baptists, a Comprehensive History, 1779-1999*, Albert Wardin writes that Folk knew his stands for prohibition of alcoholic beverages and for organized convention work caused the loss of some subscribers. His own health may have been on Folk's mind.

Albert R. Bond, 1917-1920

Albert R. Bond stepped forward to buy the paper, and to take over as owner and editor. A native of Wilson County, Tennessee, Bond had served as pastor for several churches in the South, including Franklin, Tennessee. He had written books and booklets, and one was *The Master Preacher — A Study of the Homiletics of Jesus*. Murphy Cooper of Chattanooga bought the *Baptist and Reflector* from Bond in 1920, having a background in secular writing and as a pastor in several churches. He was a first-year student at Southern Baptist Theological Seminary when Bond was a senior. They knew each other.

Bond became editorial secretary of the Southern Baptist Education Board in Birmingham, Alabama, for seven years. He served later as assistant manager with the *Daily Independent*, also in Birmingham, and continued writing.

Homer L. Grice perhaps explained this transitional period of time in the 125th anniversary issue of the *Baptist and Reflector* in January 1959. Grice was a member of the Southern Baptist Historical Commission, Nashville. His article about the paper and its editors included some little known information.

Grice wrote, "In 1917 Albert R. Bond bought Folk's interest. Then M.R. Cooper bought the paper and edited it until he sold it to the Tennessee Baptist Convention in 1921." But Bond in his brief stint as editor could not overcome financial problems. He had to

Albert Bond

sell, and Cooper was the buyer. He too was unable to overcome that same problem. He had sold his home and poured his personal finances into the purchase, to no avail. Though he was editor and owner for less than a year, he was outspoken in his editorial remarks.

[Editor's note: The *B&R* bound volume containing most of Bond's tenure as editor is in very poor condition. But a few examples of his work were salvaged.]

During his time, Southern Baptists were engaged in a fund-raising effort, striving to raise $75 Million Campaign. The papers of state Baptist conventions were heavily involved in the program.

The front page of October 9, 1919, bore an attractive banner promoting the campaign. This issue contains lengthy articles by well-known Baptist leaders, writing about varied applications of the project. G.S. Dobbins wrote about "The Heart of Enlistment," stating that "… This is enlistment, converting unused assets into available resources. It is the single greatest task in the $75 Million Campaign. It is far more vital … than raising the money at which we aim. Paul meant just this when he gave the reason for the astonishing liberality of the Macedonian Christians that they first

gave of themselves to the Lord, and to us through the will of God."
Other articles also pointed to the necessity of enlistment of the
entire church body.

Making an apology, 1919 — Bond editorially apologized to subscribers for recent tardiness of delivery. "This has been due to the
great volume of business in the Nashville post office, and also to
the fact that our printers have been swamped with other work, so
many churches promoting the $75 Million Campaign."

Thanking the churches, 1919 — "We are thankful that during
the past few weeks eighty-five churches came into the budget plan
of the *Baptist and Reflector* for every family. It is a new day for
these churches. ... Each member will learn how to be a real co-
worker."

A Day for the Called, 1919 — "The new calendar of Baptist effort
will have another Red Letter Day. Baptists are now in the midst of
the greatest six months in their history. The days are filled with
stirring calls to service. The days are large with possibilities. The
eyes of the world are turned toward Southern Baptists as never
before. The air is filled with expectancy. The month of October is
designated for enlistment. October (brings) another Red Letter Day.
Calling out the Called will be emphasized. Each church should seek
to bring to public recognition those who will accept certain places
of service in the church because they shall have felt the call of God.
... There should be decisions of thousands of young men and
women to give themselves to missionary and other definite forms
of church work, according as God may impress them with their
duty. ... Make preparations for the day and come to it expecting
God to call out those whom He has already called for special
services."

Presumptuous Faith, 1919 — We are warned against presumptuous sins. We are not warned against a presumptuous faith. Such
faith would mean confidence in God though every reasonable
expectation might oppose such a faith. These days of great soul
stress challenge Southern Baptists to presumptuous faith, a faith
that overlooks seemingly impassable barriers and attempts duties
that seem impassable. The very essence of faith is the willingness to
walk the unknown path, to reach out into the dark with confidence
to obey fully when obedience may mean sacrifice and intellectual
uncertainty. ... The invitation that Jesus gave for answered prayer

measured not for the results as such, but the relation of the results to faith.

A World Neighborhood, 1919 — The ends of the earth have come together. The war (World War I) has brought every country before the gaze of the whole world. Provincialism is a thing of the past. Men have become world citizens. The whole world is a great big neighborhood in which problems that disturb one class of citizens are not only observed by every other class, but in a measure the whole neighborhood. ... A strike of longshoremen in New York or by coal miners reaches beyond the payroll of these workers and becomes a national and world problem. ... As citizens of a world we must act upon the principles of world service. ... He who said, "Go ye into all the world" also said, "Lo, I am with you always."

Chastening a president 1919 — Editor Bond took issue with President Woodrow Wilson. The President vetoed a bill sent to him by Congress, which would keep wartime prohibition (liquor) in place. Wilson's veto would reopen saloons which had been closed during wartime. When the bill was sent back to Congress, both houses quickly overturned the veto. Wilson threatened to declare that since the war was over the law was not in effect, and so the saloons could reopen. Bond wrote, "We are glad Congress has set itself against any effort that would return the liquor curse to this country."

Saying Goodbye, 1920 — Three years of hard but joyful service. It has been my privilege to visit practically every section of Tennessee, to meet thousands of Baptists. ... I have not been unmindful of the heritage of years before me (Folk's editorship)... my commanding desire has been to make religion seem more a real experience that should express itself in the largest possible service to the Lord. ... At the Executive Board meeting April 20, it was decided not to purchase the paper. It became necessary for someone to finance the paper, who could take care of any problem or possible loss.

Murphy R. Cooper, 1920-21

When Murphy Cooper succeeded Albert Bond as editor, he realized that the road out of financial difficulty would be rough. He hoped to succeed, and the TBC Executive Board also wanted a financially sound paper.

Cooper soon displayed his writing skills, and being frank with subscribers, about the dire circumstances. He was ready to speak up on issues of that era.

For example, in an editorial differing with popular opinions of many men, he maintained that women had equal rights in preaching, praying, and speaking in public assemblies and in teaching men. He also spoke out during the furor about women's right to vote. The Tennessee legislature's vote in 1920 for ratifying the 19th Amendment gave women the right to vote. Cooper said, "Three Cheers for Tennessee," and also wrote that woman's suffrage was a God-given right. He added, "If the women will use

M.R. Cooper

this right in helping to solve the moral and educational questions, they will have their reward."

For the paper's front-page motto, Cooper chose: "Lovingly wooing men while unsparingly condemning their sins." In his first editorial he gave assurance to readers of his belief in a good denominational paper. And the editorial was an honest assessment of the need for more support — more readers and more income.

"In becoming editor of the *Baptist and Reflector* I am not unmindful of the superhuman task and the great responsibility. The *Baptist and Reflector* is an old and honorable institution, established by men of keen minds and charming personalities." He wrote of meeting Folk and Bond earlier, and of his admiration of both men. "They have made the *Baptist and Reflector* a great power for good for Tennessee Baptists, and I take up the task they have laid down. The Tennessee Baptists ... are kings and priests in the household of faith ... .

"First, the new editor will endeavor to give the news that will be of interest to the Baptists of Tennessee. Fleetwood Ball will continue his notes, 'Among the Brethren,' and I want every pastor and school man in Tennessee to write the news every week and send it to me. ... But remember that white paper is scarce and high, so write briefly. ... I pledge to promote education in general and Baptist education in particular. Union University, Carson-

Newman College, Tennessee College, and Hall-Moody may expect full and impartial support … .

"I stand four-square for missions, city, state, home and foreign, and orphanages, aged ministers, and every cause fostered by Southern Baptists.

"The editor and the paper are independent. (My) parents and forebears for 300 years have been Baptists of the Calvinistic, Puritan type. Just to save the readers a stamp and my time to reply in the future, let me say here that I do not approve of alien immersion. Baptism should be regular and biblical, but it should not be made a test of fellowship."

Cooper then again asked readers to write him: "If you write well on a subject of interest and importance you will get a check before very long.

"It takes both brains and money to make a good newspaper, and it requires no small amount of both to pull one out of a hole and place it on a rock foundation. ... The *Baptist and Reflector* has been a power for good among Tennessee Baptists for many years. This paper is recognized by all Southern Baptist editors as an established and conservative journal, one of the best. This good old packhorse has been staggering under denominational burdens for several months, and in his weakness fell into a financial ditch.

"To be a good Samaritan I have sold my home and placed every dollar and whatever business ability I may have inherited or developed in this paper. ... Everyone who will help the new editor out of the ditch with the *Baptist and Reflector* and the consolidated will be a good Samaritan, and will insure a better newspaper for Tennessee Baptists."

The honesty displayed by Cooper and his depth of concern for the life of the paper were not sufficient. Finally, he had to sell the paper to the Tennessee Baptist Convention on January 4, 1921.

Hight C. Moore, 1921

Here's what happened next. Hight C. Moore, one of the directors elected for the newly purchased paper, was editor for the last weeks of January 1921 as requested by the Executive Board, Tennessee Baptist Convention. When the board met in early January, action was taken to purchase the paper. The board named directors for the new member of the family. Part of the action stated, "... The directors hope to be able to announce the name of the permanent editor at an early date." The permanent editor, his brother, Jesse Daniel Moore, began as editor in March 1921.

In the January 4 issue of the *Baptist and Reflector*, there was a full report of the Executive Board's action. The paper reported that the board unanimously agreed "... the purchase price should be $15,000, provided a satisfactory adjustment could be made with the creditors so as to deliver the *Baptist and Reflector* free of all debt..."

In his first editorial he reminded readers of the strong history of the paper, and noted that the purchase gave it new owners [See Chapter Five]. Hight Moore later was editorial secretary of the Baptist Sunday School Board.

A national movement, which effected the paper during this period, involved a Southern Baptist Convention effort in fund raising. At the SBC annual meeting in 1919, a report was adopted: "In view of the needs of the world at this hour, in view of the numbers and ability of Southern Baptists, we suggest that in the organized work of this Convention we undertake to raise not less than $75 million in five years." W. Fred Kendall wrote that the urgency of the campaign was prompted by the bloody battles of World War I. "The horrors of the world war convinced Southern Baptists of the weakness of civilization that was unchristianized. ... They came to realize, as they never had realized before, that in spite of the fact that the world war had been fought for democracy, the conditions that came immediately following the war jeopardized all true democracy unless the world was given a spiritual democracy ... ."

Tennessee's goal was $4 million and Tennessee Baptists eventually reached almost eighty-three percent of the goal. It was believed that ownership of the paper would enable the Convention to have more publicity for the campaign. Thus the paper became the Convention's official newsjournal.

In a period of two years (1919-20) six more Southern Baptist state conventions bought their papers. Denominational consolidation and convention ownership and widespread financial uneasiness were determining factors.

B its of Biography, Albert R. Bond — Native of Wilson County, Tennessee, born March 9 1874; earned three degrees from

Peabody College and ThM. degree from Southern Baptist Theological Seminary; served as pastor of eight churches in Mississippi, Kentucky, Ohio, Georgia, and Tennessee; edited *Baptist and Reflector* 1917-20, later editorial secretary of Southern Baptist Education Board, management with Birmingham *Daily Independent* and Southern Radio News; authored several books; married to Ruth Pugh who died 1914, one son, Richmond Pugh; married Catherine Walmsey.

B its of Biography, Murphy R. Cooper — Born in Scott County, Mississippi; educated at Southwest Baptist College and Southern Baptist Theological Seminary; had early experience as business manager for his father's business; correspondent for *Commercial Appeal* newspaper and Crowell Publishing Company (magazines); married Garrie Smith; they had four sons; served in the ministry twenty years, and later operated book stores in Richmond, Va., and Pulaski, Va., where he died.

B its of Biography, Hight C. Moore — Globe, North Carolina, was his birthplace; given leave of absence from duties as editorial secretary, Baptist Sunday School Board, to serve as acting editor, *Baptist and Reflector;* named as a director for the paper when it was bought by the Executive Board, Tennessee Baptist Convention, 1921; brother of J.D. Moore who was named editor that year.

CHAPTER FIVE

J. D. Moore
O. E. Bryan
Beginning Again
1921-25

L iving through an era of financial turmoil and indecision, Tennessee Baptist leaders were wary of the future of the *Baptist and Reflector*. There was concern — the paper finally had become the dependable bright star for Tennessee Baptists. But difficulties continued during the 1917-21 period despite valiant efforts by editors and supporters. When Murphy Cooper bought the paper from Albert Bond in 1920, he described the paper's condition as "stepping into a deep financial hole." He was right. The "hole" was getting deeper.

Editor and paper would need help in getting out of that hole. Despite selling his home and throwing all of his assets into a plan of survival, he too was forced to sell.

So this chapter of the *Baptist and Reflector's* life depicts the first years of convention ownership of a paper with a reliable reputation, but with a need for financial stability. Though most previous editors favored private ownership, rescue by the Tennessee Baptist Convention was the first step to a lasting solution.

Sensing the need to give some stability of ownership, the Executive Board of the Tennessee Baptist Convention purchased the paper from Cooper. Ownership also carries with it a measure of control. Ownership guarantees a steady flow of Baptist news, whereas previous editors and owners had a global and often secular view of some content. Political and civic news were used. In the early years such news helped readers to be aware of worldwide events, and when counted in inches, helped fill the pages. There were no ready sources of news such as Baptist Press, daily newspapers, magazines, computers, and other electronic means of distribution.

Jesse D. Moore, 1921-25

As explained earlier, the Executive Board appointed directors for the new arrangement and asked Hight C. Moore to edit the paper on an interim basis. And in March 1921, Jesse D. Moore took over the helm of the *Baptist and Reflector*. He was the first to lead the official newsjournal owned and operated by the Tennessee Baptist Convention. The North Carolina native had been a pastor and denominational worker.

"The *Baptist and Reflector* has had a long and honorable history," Jesse Moore wrote in his first editorial, "It began eighty-five

Jesse D. Moore

years ago as *THE BAPTIST.* Fifty years ago the *Baptist and Reflector* entered upon its career. Thirty-five years ago the consolidation of the two papers was effected and for three and a half decades the combined journal has served its day and generation. All the while it has been under private control, but now it passes into the hands directly of the denomination. May it be that the organ of Tennessee Baptists will enter a sphere of ever larger service than in the past."

In a November 1921 issue Moore paid tribute to former editor Edgar Folk. The paper announced the coming Tennessee Baptist Convention in Nashville, and named the city's churches and pastors. It noted there were thirteen Baptist churches in Nashville. The paper also announced entertainment during the event according to the "Harvard Plan" with guests supplied room and breakfast, the local ladies serving the midday meal to messengers. Local chairman O.L. Hailey told messengers they would be met at the trains.

Moore gave the paper a different look, with a clear, crisp layout. Use of photographs was somewhat limited, perhaps because of lack of skilled photography and costs. But he made attractive use of "cuts" of paintings, which illustrated biblical scenes. The paper began to shift toward a modern look, attractive to prospective readers.

On the front page of the paper's July 7, 1921, issue, Moore placed a large picture of Carson-Newman College, "where the Bible Conference is to be held." Four brief "opinion pieces" were used also. One paid tribute to The Preacher's Wife —

"In reading the biography of Dr. J.R. Gambrell, one is impressed with the prominence of that silent, quiet influence which was exerted upon his life by his companion; she who bore his children and upon whom domestic responsibilities fell with direct and unceasing force; she who 'remained with the stuff' should share equally with him 'who went afield.' We are therefore disposed to regard the name of J.B. Gambrell as the composite of two lives. And as it was in that case, so may it be in many another.

"Honor to that host of preachers' wives who cheerfully endure the privations of a frequent change of residence, and who go uncomplaining to their daily household duties which are multiplied to them by scant incomes and the husband's constant absence from home; they are the bravest warriors that ever fought the battle of life!"

Quotes from Moore and other editors reveal a certain eloquence, almost formality, in word usage. Sentences often were lengthy, and editors from the paper's earlier years assumed readers could store away the news from issue to issue. For instance, editorials referred simply to "Stockholm," the Convention meeting, the Bible Conference, etc., without identifying properly. And of course, the King James Version was the only version used. Even ordinary news stories were laden with personal viewpoints and opinions, such as, "He is of the finest type of Christian gentleman, devoted pastor, and Gospel preacher. His people are loyal to him and help to crown his efforts with success." Like his predecessors, Moore's writing style was eloquent.

Two pages of "Contributions" collected and/or written by O.L. Hailey are found in that July 1921 issue. Hailey, son-in-law of J.R. Graves, addressed a spiritual security thought, and called his idea, "Put No One but Americans on Guard Tonight." He addressed an article in another paper, written by "a well-known and prominent leader," who said, "... Most of us believe that we have conserved all the wisdom and discoveries of the past, and that our great seers have a clearer vision and a deeper insight than those in former ages."

Hailey had referred to George Washington's command to his troops that they should always be on guard, and beware of the English. Washington alerted those soldiers who were loyal because so much was at stake. Others in the ranks were serving, but did not have as much at stake. Hailey concluded his message with this: "The purpose of this article is to arouse our leaders, and especially our editors, to be on their guard, and save the people from the blight of such utterly un-Christian propaganda. Put none but loyal men on guard now."

In the same issue Moore addressed the power of the famous English pastor, Charles Spurgeon, as a leading Baptist of his era, and also the evils of divorce. "With what appalling frequency is the marriage bond legally broken!" Moore wrote, "With what intrepidity do parties to such action seek release from the sacred ties. And with what apparent indifference to all consequences do most of us witness the orgy of divorces! We have no single greater evil. ... The divorce mill grinds too fast, but let us proclaim aloud the remedy for the malady, of which it is merely a symptom, and that remedy is the religion of Jesus Christ in the home."

Editorially he also twice reminded subscribers, "More than $10,000 are due the *Baptist and Reflector* by subscribers. Please look at your label and see if you are among that number. We will greatly appreciate immediate attention to this."

Some editorial samples:

World Baptists and world peace, 1923 — (Editor's note: Fallout from World War I was still widespread.) In the program of the Baptist World Alliance, the consideration of international peace is assigned an important and strategic place. ... The impact of the great gathering at Stockholm should be felt throughout Europe and should mightily make for amity among all the nations of the world. Statesmen have met in vain, Versailles, Washington, Genoa, Lausanne, and other conferences of world diplomats have brought forth no solution of international problems, and have presented no acceptable remedy for the deep-seated anguish of war-weary nations. Democracy is the prevailing trend among all nations now. Political independence is more than many of them know what to do with, but they all want it. ... Religious freedom is the counterpart of political democracy. ... A democracy which does not function in time of war needs to be remodeled, or else to have its laws regarding war revised.

Evolution Legislation, 1923 — The law which is now before the Tennessee legislature proposing to make it unlawful to teach evolution in any of the public schools of the state, should be supported by all Christian people. ... Legislation cannot function in any matter involving Christian faith; either in support of or in opposition to, this or that belief as such. The State cannot dictate in matters of conscience to its citizens. It cannot therefore sanction that which trespasses upon the consciences of any.

Fundamental Sunday School Lessons, 1923 — The World's Fundamental Conference held its first session at Fort Worth, Texas, last week, and ... made plans for the establishment of an independent Sunday School Lesson System, breaking relations with the International Committee and also with all denominational publishers using the International Uniform Lessons. Thus the divisive character of the organization, inter-denominational, independent, self-styled 'Fundamentalist' movement actually shows up, statements by Baptist Bible Union advocates to the contrary notwithstanding. ... In the Sunday School Board we have all the equipment and plant necessary for a great denominational service. It exists solely to minister the interests of Southern Baptists and through them to Kingdom causes everywhere. ... Baptists of the South ought to control their own Sunday School publications. We have no need nor occasion to let it out to anybody else whomsoever."

The front page of June 7, 1923, contained several bits of wisdom and two editorials:

Cheap sensationalism — Cheap sensationalism first attracts, then disappoints, then disgusts. The truth of this has been tested so often that it is not worth while for any preacher to make further experiments. [Moore's words were noteworthy then — and now.]

A timely warning — G.P. Bostick, Southern Baptist missionary to China, writes, "It looks to me that at home and in the mission fields, we as Baptists, are losing power by stressing mental and physical training more that rebirth and 'growth in the knowledge and grace of our Lord Jesus Christ.' " He said also "… the world must avoid falling into Germany's great error in stressing mental education and culture so much more than heart change and growth."

The King James Version — For popular study, or in devotional reading, the King James, or the "Authorized" version of the Bible was never in greater favor than now; not only because of its usefulness in the past but more especially because of its usefulness in at the present. … We do not object to the use of [other] such versions as linguistic sidelights on the Word of God, or the opinions of eminent scholars as to the meaning of biblical language, but we are unready to accept any of them as the best text of the Scriptures for common use." [The ongoing discussions of Bible translations were evident before, during, and after Moore's tenure at the *Baptist and Reflector*.]

Brutality in football, 1924 — We are not a judge of athletics and we do not wish to set ourself up as arbiter concerning the morals of modern intercollegiate games, but we have an ordinary discernment of what is dangerous especially when we see the list of casualties. In recent games between colleges in the state, serious injuries and death have resulted from the playing of football. … It is the physical peril in it that gives zest to the contest. It is the presence of danger which calls for such precision and quick judgment in playing as makes the game scientific and educational — a merit it would not have if the possibility of danger were reduced and the game resolved into what the rough and tumble athletes would regard as a tame affair.

(Moore ended the editorial with a suggestion that game rules be revised or that "our denominational schools be told by the denomination that Baptist boys are not sent to them to be maimed or slaughtered on the field of sport." When he was editor earlier, Albert Bond also said the sport was brutal, even urging Vanderbilt University to drop it.)

An advertisement in the October 2, 1924, issue of the paper claimed a cure for cancer. The ad from Kellam Hospital Inc., Richmond, Virginia, stated, "The Kellam Hospital cures cancers, tumor, ulcer, X-ray burns, and chronic sores without the use of the knife, X-ray, radium, acids, or serum and we have cured over ninety percent of the many hundreds of sufferers treated during the past twenty-three years.

Almost as unbelievable is an ad in December 1924: "An automobile goes twenty-seven miles on air by using an automatic device which was installed in less than five minutes. The automobile was making thirty miles on a gallon of gasoline but after this remarkable invention was installed, it made better than fifty-seven. The inventor, Mr. J.A. Stransky (address given) wants agents and is willing to send a sample at his own risk. Write him today." (That kind of boasting would attract much attention in 2005!)

Harry Clark, education secretary, had some interesting advice in the March 1, 1923 paper, "How Some Boys Earn Money to Go to School" —

"The American boy who is ambitious can generally find a way to keep himself in school. Here are some of the ways some boys have worked their way through school. — Picking fruit, husking corn, gathering nuts, picking cotton, cleaning yards, washing windows, varnishing chairs, running errands, waxing floors, cleaning sidewalks, caring for furnaces, mowing and raking lawns, sifting and dumping ashes, making syrup, decorating show windows, tutoring backward students, beating carpets and rugs, sawing and cutting wood, working about a dairy, cleaning cellars, attics, and barns; painting houses, barns and fences ..." and many more.

Editor Moore addressed "Patriotic Secret Orders" in the March 15, 1923, issue —

We are not a member of any secret society. But it should be said that an organization which is composed only of Americans and aims only to preserve American ideals should be preferred by both the religious and daily press to another order which is based on allegiance to a foreign potentate, but which wants to feed on American bounty. However, "Americanism" will save nobody; a society of pureblood Americans may be far from being an "assembly of the First Born." The kind of Americanism, which deserves to be perpetrated, is that which consists of "pure and undefiled religion before God and the Father." The Evangelical churches are our best patriotic organizations. Let the Roman Catholic Church be regarded as un-American only so far as it is anti-Christian.

An ad in that issue was selling army shoes for $2.75, the shoes "are selling fast" and "pay postman on receipt of goods or send money order" to the U.S. Stores Co., 1441 Broadway, New York City.

A half-page portrait of President Warren Gamaliel Harding carried this caption: "His last public utterances as President of the United States were a plea for the spirit of Christ among all mankind. No purer man ever held the highest office in the land. In the after-glow of the sunset of his life, let all the peoples, wrapped in silence, meditate upon God who alone made him good and who only can make a nation great."

Jesse Moore told the subscribers of his retirement on the editorial page, January 15, 1925. He reported that he was leaving the editor's post on his fourth anniversary in the post. However, Wardin wrote that Moore left for a position with the Baptist Sunday School Board. Moore closed his remarks, "Far more than he (Moore) deserves, his readers have been considerate and appreciative; and the ties of friendship which of necessity have been largely invisible are to be cherished as one of the strongest endearments of life." On March 1 he wrote that John D. Freeman had been asked to follow him, and hoped he would answer positively, and soon.

O.E. Bryan, March 19 - May 28, 1925

Freeman accepted but there was an interim before he took

Oscar E. Bryan

office. It was not unusual for an Executive Board staff member to fill such a brief vacancy. Oscar E. Bryan, corresponding secretary (executive director) served as editor from March 19 to May 28, 1925.

Bryan announced this move in the March 19 issue — "The Corresponding Secretary of the Executive Board of the Tennessee Baptist Convention for a brief time is acting as editor of the *Baptist and Reflector*. ... While we are under this burden we ask the patience, sympathy, and prayers of our people."

Bryant had been elected Corresponding Secretary beginning in November 1924, and held that post until 1933.

On the front of his first edition, Bryan placed the names of Memphis hotels accommodating messengers to the May 13-17 Southern Baptist Convention. Room prices ranged from $1.00 per day up to $3.50. He noted that "All who desire reservation in private homes, where entertainment will be furnished at the rate of $1.50 per day for lodging and breakfast" and gave the name of the chairman of such housing.

The "modern" era was causing havoc among Baptists in some ways. The Beulah Association spoke against "unchaperoned" car rides. The Dyer County Association said, "By many, the improper use of the automobile is thought to be the outstanding moral and social evil of the day. By improper use is meant speeding, reckless driving, petting parties, transporting illegal products, and breaking up the home by keeping the members of the family separated continually."

Dancing was condemned also. Oscar Bryan wrote an editorial for the April 16, 1925 edition, speaking against dancing, and saying it was a menace to individuals, and "… it weakens the individual's resistance to subtle temptations and takes the keen edge off of modesty and innocent refinement." The editorial said, "The dance cultivates that which is lowest in the human race. It tends toward abnormal development of the sexual nature." He also wrote that "Dancing members weaken the spiritually of the church."

In his dual leadership role, Bryan introduced Tennessee Baptists to the new Cooperative Program in 1925. The CP idea followed the conclusion of the Seventy-five Million Campaign. The CP posed the genius of providing a unified program of financial support for all TBC and SBC institutions and programs.

Evidently some Tennessee Baptists wanted to know whether Bryan was receiving additional salary while serving as editor and corresponding secretary. Bryan responded editorially, assuring readers that he did not get a second salary. He added that he was able to take on the responsibility. Bryan said goodbye to his editor's job in one of his last editorials, saying, "We sincerely believe that in John D. Freeman our paper now has the greatest editor in the Southern Baptist Convention."

B its of Biography, Jesse D. Moore — Born April 23, 1873, Globe, North Carolina; graduate of Wake Forest College 1893; attended Southern Baptist Theological Seminary one year; pastor of several churches in North Carolina and two in South Carolina; was first Sunday School Secretary for South Carolina Baptist Convention seven years; first full-time BYPU secretary for North Carolina State Board four years; general manager Ridgecrest Baptist Assembly; first *B&R* editor under Executive Board; later on editorial staff for Baptist Sunday School Board; married America Brown, they had six children.

Bits of Biography, Oscar E. Bryan — Born in Mississippi August 4, 1873; called Memphis his home; graduated Baylor University and Southwestern Baptist Theological Seminary; received DD degrees from Baylor and Georgetown (Kentucky) College, and LL.D from Union University; evangelist with SWBTS; pastor in Waco, Texas; secretary of Kentucky Baptist State Board; headed department of evangelism and enlistment Home Mission Board, and executive secretary Tennessee Baptist Convention. Married Fannie Elizabeth Davidson, who helped originate the Sunbeam Band and edited Baptist literature. He died January 24, 1934.

CHAPTER SIX

Tennessee Baptist Convention More Involved
John D. Freeman
1925-33

John D. Freeman was pastor of Belmont Heights Baptist Church in Nashville when called to follow Jesse D. Moore as editor of the *Baptist and Reflector*. His background included service as pastor of several other churches and as a missionary in the Ozark Mountains. After twelve years with the paper, he was named executive secretary of the Tennessee Baptist Convention. He was well known in TBC circles.

Freeman's leadership as editor coincided with Oscar E. Bryan, the convention's executive secretary. These were crucial years for Tennessee Baptists.

Both men had a flair for leadership. Albert Wardin, writing in *Tennessee Baptists, a Comprehensive History, 1779-1999,* points to Freeman, Bryan, and Oury W. Taylor, as dominant forces in the Tennessee Baptist Convention. Freeman was editor of the paper when Bryan was executive secretary, and when Freeman followed Bryan as executive secretary, Taylor became editor.

Wardin wrote, "Three leaders with strong conservative convictions — Oscar Bryan, John Freeman, and Oury Taylor — dominated Tennessee Baptist life from 1924 to 1942. Their careful leadership helped meet the challenges of the hour and laid the basis for future advance. ... Their mutual relationships, pastoral experience, roots in the rural South, common touch and common sense, theological convictions, and continuity in office provided steady leadership."

Freeman and Taylor wrote vigorously and fearlessly, according to Wardin, in the tradition of Graves and Folk, and both had strong theological focus that gave confidence and direction to the TBC. Further, both editors used the paper in forging support for "a coordinated denominational program."

Freeman seized the moment. From the outset, Tennessee Baptists realized he was capable for the task ahead. On the first editorial page, June 4, 1925, he let readers know that the paper would be an instrument of cooperation and strength for the Tennessee Baptist Convention. He greeted the Baptist family, expressing his feelings about leaving the pastorate, while realizing his duties as editor. He answered two questions put to himself and the readers — What is the *Baptist and Reflector*? and, How may we have a great paper?

He answered the first question by agreeing that the paper is an organ of the Tennessee Baptist Convention — and as such, the organ "should promulgate Baptist views and principles. ... Any matters that touch and influence the life and work of the Baptists of Tennessee and that touch and influence the ministry of Baptists where Tennessee Baptists are concerned, thus become material for publication ... ." In his answer to the second question, Freeman wrote, "The *Baptist and Reflector* is more than a paper, it is an institution organized for the purpose of ministering to the spiritual needs of a great host of people ... it belongs to the Baptists of Tennessee."

Then he made four points for subscribers: they must read the paper, they must support the paper, they can help by being patient and sympathetic with the paper and the editor, and they must remember "that the editor is a minister of God and that He has not severed His relationship to the work of the Kingdom." He added, "With all the Baptists of Tennessee supporting the paper, it will become a mighty factor in the denominational life of the state and of the world. To that end, the editor pledges his heart, his mind, his brain, his very life."

The new editor was not alone in his comparison of pastor and editor. Previous editors had come to the position after serving as pastors. Freeman referred to the changes from one to the other. "Pastors will appreciate the feelings of fear, misgiving, longing, heartache, etc., that have come during the weeks while the matter of becoming editor of the *Baptist and Reflector* has been under

consideration. Indeed, the change has been painful. ... However, the editor understands full well that change is needful ... there will be ample compensation for the losses occasioned by the change in fields of service."

From the outset, Freeman often used snippets of news, advice, and opinion on the editorial page. He was a gifted speaker and denominational leader. Like most Baptist pastors he also enjoyed good humor. He is the only *Baptist and Reflector* editor who later was named executive secretary of the Convention.

John D. Freeman

Here are some examples of wisdom, humor, and news:

• Nearly two million aliens, many of them low-class southern Europeans, are knocking at our doors for admission. Let no voter relent in his demands upon our congressmen to maintain the present restrictions against immigration. Every new laborer admitted to our land now robs an American of his job in a time of great hardships.

• The worst thing about the radio is the songs it has brought into being.

• We need not be so sorely troubled about our denominational debts. Progress is sometimes made when we go backwards. Retrenchment now may mean economies in the future and somehow economy is the note that needs to be sounded everywhere from President Coolidge down to the smallest farmer and mechanic.

• Faith is the lever which pries open God's storehouse.

• Some day our pastors are going to realize what some of them have discovered to be true: the state paper is worth ten times as much as a little bulletin. Yet the bulletin as a rule costs them as much as the paper would.

• The editor does not believe that he needs to apologize for the many typographical errors that occur in the letters that go out from the office to readers of the paper. In addition to all other duties, he is his own stenographer and many times must dash off the letters as rapidly as his fingers will work, and turn to other duties without a chance to read what he has written. This explanation is sent out, lest somebody blames a stenographer who "is not."

• Many a bold prophet has been branded as a carping critic.

• The Fox movie magnates made a bad break when they announced their "Movie Church Service." The very next week bankruptcy proceedings were begun against them. We know churches that have gone the same way because of their spiritless and mechanical services.

• Jealousy is the deadly poison in the cup of marital harmony.

• Go to church. God isn't going to hold you responsible for the kind of sermon you hear.

• Some of our pastors need to get out on the big highway construction jobs and learn from the engineers how obstacles are overcome through faith and works combined.

• If you have lost your faith, go back into the mountains this summer and spend two weeks with some blessed old saint in a revival meeting where folks still believe that God leads his people in a supernatural way.

• It is a lot wiser for one to spend his time thinking about what he is going to do when Jesus comes, than it is to spend time thinking about when Jesus is coming.

• Honorary degrees are very like vaccination sores on little children; no matter how many of the crowd have them, the other fellow is glad when he can boast one too.

• While we Baptists are piling up machinery at the top of our organization, Holy Rollers, Russellites, Seventh Day Adventists, and others are digging away the foundations that have made us strong for the past three centuries; namely, our rural and small town members.

Leafing through records of history, we continue to follow John Freeman's tracks as editor of the *Baptist and Reflector*. He advocated voting rights for all citizens, and wrote that legislation could never produce social equality for white or black people. He also said that legislation could give equal protection before the law and equal educational opportunities. But he didn't offer solutions. He did print an article written by Charles O'Neal, a black, who pled for recognition and justice for all. In a 1935 edition, the paper also printed an article by a Union University student favoring equal opportunities in education, housing, and jobs.

In 1929, Freeman wrote that country churches should consider consolidation and move nearer to main highways. He also believed that Home Mission workers would be helpful in the rural areas. On another subject, Freeman criticized certain citywide evangelistic meetings, holding that the speakers usually were not able to preach on the Baptist faith and fundamental beliefs. He believed the meetings often failed to unite Christian groups, and could separate them.

W. Fred Kendall, in *A History of the Tennessee Baptist Convention,* compliments Freeman's work as editor in using the paper to support TBC endeavors: "The *Baptist and Reflector* grew into the life and work of Tennessee Baptists, after it became the Convention's paper. John D. Freeman made valuable suggestions to the Convention for methods of getting people better acquainted with the paper and its ministry and work in the denomination. Financing the paper was always a problem. [Editor's note: Financing remained difficult in later years as well.] Some advertising was sold and the subscription price was kept as low as possible, to enable more people to take the paper."

It is interesting that in the paper's 170 years, the cost of an individual subscription remains low. Beginning at one or two dollars in 1835, the price now is only eleven dollars a year.

It is easy to agree with Wardin that Freeman was one of the dominant figures in the Convention during his tenure as editor and later as executive secretary (1925-42). He was forceful in his beliefs, as other editors were, and committed to defend them. During his early years as editor, the Ku Klux Klan was impacting some states, including Tennessee. It is pertinent that Freeman commented editorially that he had never been a member nor argued for its programs. He added, "The Klan numbers among its members many of the choicest American citizens." His remark came close to including Baptists among those members.

The evolution theory debacle was a thorn during Freeman's years as editor. Most Tennessee Baptists were not in favor of the theory. Earlier, editors J.R. Graves and E.E. Folk spoke out strongly, denouncing the premise of evolution, despite Charles Darwin's claims. Editor J.D. Moore in 1923 favored a Tennessee legislative bill to forbid teaching evolution in the state's schools. He supported the bill and pointed out that it could not be taught since the state prohibited teaching religion in schools. The bill was challenged and a trial in 1925 was held in Dayton, Tennessee, pitting famed attorney Clarence Darrow against the equally famous political leader William Jennings Bryan. Bryan was called as a special prosecutor, and Darrow defended John Scopes, a local teacher who was accused of teaching evolution. The jury found Scopes guilty, but the verdict was overturned on appeal. A few days after the trial, Bryan died. In many minds, Darrow, a relentless lawyer, was the cause of Bryan's death.

The whole affair was a media circus and news reporters from across the nation were on hand to report. Freeman was not left behind. He ably depicted Bryan as a Christian martyr, and the paper carried news and editorials during the trial. Freeman wrote fiery editorials, claiming that the trial was "the beginning of the battle between the beast and the Sons of God." He challenged newspapers that wrote unkindly about Bryan. One of his editorials claimed that "Christ's Greatest Champion Has Fallen."

Like some of his predecessors, Freeman was not reticent in opposing other church bodies. The paper opposed the candidacy of Alfred E. Smith when he was seeking the Democratic nomination. In an August 1926 issue, Freeman wrote an anti–Smith article opposing his candidacy, and began a series later that year with the same opposition. Smith was a Catholic, and to Freeman and others, that was sufficient reason to oppose his nomination.

Giving some good advice for every generation, John Freeman addressed some of the problems during the Great Depression of the early 1930s. He advised that individuals should economize, and not lose hope for better times, spend less on their own selfish interests, and return to the farm, which would help provide food and a more peaceful spiritual life (*Baptist and Reflector*, June 9, 1932).

From the editorial pages of John D. Freeman, these are samples:
Information wanted, 1925 — The editor is anxious to ascertain just what Tennessee Baptists want their paper to be. Therefore, he

is making this public appeal for 1,000 readers to write him a short letter setting forth their ideas as to the very best way to make the paper a readable and helpful publication. Let the letters be brief, certainly not more than 150 or 200 words. The information received will be tabulated and published for the information of other editors. Let pastors, laymen, women, and the young people send in their suggestions at once.

Editorial Note, 1925 — The person who says, "I don't see no use in sending money to heathen countries when we have so many heathens here at home" is usually the one who never tries to convert the heathen anywhere. Usually, when one becomes interested in the heathen abroad, he soon becomes interested in the lost nearby.

Editorial Note, 1925 — The less power an automobile has, the more noise it makes. The same thing is true of many people. And whenever one hears a church member who boasts and grumbles and fusses, he may be sure he is in the presence of a powerless Christian, or else has run afoul of a hypocrite.

Editorial Note, 1925 — If our Baptist churches would spend more time in real prayer and less time in social amusements, we would find it less difficult to "get into the spirit of the Lord." In all too many of our churches prayer has been reduced to the merest formality, while the social features of our services have been magnified to the Nth degree.

Editorial Note, 1925 — For the sake of the brethren who had to be neglected last week, we wish to make the following explanation: We just do not have space to print all the matter that comes to us. And it is all good, too. We cannot accept advertising and then refuse to use it. ... We urge our correspondents to be sparing with their space. We are shelving all the great long articles possible. We are seeking short, newsy articles and good doctrinal articles, and they are coming in. ... Do not write out long reports of revival meetings. ... Do not send in programs that already have been rendered. ... Remember that the *Baptist and Reflector* charges one cent per word for all formal resolutions. ... We cannot deviate from this rule in favor of any church or individual. ... Let all pastors who wish to report their Sunday services on the conference page send twenty-five cents to us for a pack of report blanks. ... Write your article on the typewriter if you can get access to one. Never write on but one side of the paper, and use double spacing. ... Get a copy of R.B. Nieses's *News Writing for Religious Workers*, and study it carefully. We will be glad to send you one for $1.25.

Editorial Note, 1930 — We had another war (WW I) and now it is taking seventy-two cents out of every dollar of income our national government has to pay our war debts. President (Herbert) Hoover is unafraid and in his recent report showed that of the budget of nearly four billions of dollars which has been made up for 1930, almost three-fourths of it goes to pay on our war debts. Well, if folks will fight, they just have to suffer.

Front page advertisement, 1930 — Editor Freeman wrote on page one, January 16 edition: "This issue of the paper is sent forth on the eve of the annual Automobile Show which will be held in the Hippodrome, Nashville, January 25. Grateful acknowledgement is made for the courtesy of the Nashville firms who have patronized our advertising columns in this issue, and we sincerely hope our readers will not forget them when they need the services they can give." More than half the page told about the auto show, enhanced by a quarter-page picture of a new 1930 Buick, "one of the latest designs in automobiles." It cost $1,330.

Editorial note, 1930 — The temperance (anti-alcohol) forces have taken a tremendous forward stride in the production of "Deliverance," a great prohibition moving picture. Already it is in big demand, and it is reported that Premier Mussolini of Italy has asked to have the use of it in Rome. A dozen great dramatic pictures will do more than a thousand lecturers to reach the masses.

Editorial, At it again, 1930 — Some of our denominational leaders are at work early this time in order to bring about the election of their friend to the presidency of the Southern Baptist Convention. Reports show that they are using the mails for the purpose of aligning their forces and of enlisting their agencies in the campaign. With the audacity of secular politicians, they do not hesitate to engage in such a movement, for evidently they consider that matters of grave moment are at stake. ... We may be young, but we know one thing for certain; our so-called leaders would not care so much about who is going to be president of the Convention if they believed that the Holy Spirit had a chance to lead in the actions of that body.

Special edition — Editor Freeman published a ninety-two page Progress and Good Will edition of the *Baptist and Reflector* for

March 6, 1930. A large "cut" of O.E. Bryan, executive secretary, was on the front page. Words of gratitude and best wishes were used in advertisements throughout, some from political leaders. Purpose of the special emphasis was to publicize the work of the Convention and its agencies and program. Bryan's short editorial message said, "If all of our churches would only give in a reasonable way to the Cooperative Program, we would go forward in good will toward all nations of the earth and every needy cause in the homeland. This would be progress. Let us go forward."

A month earlier, Freeman expressed his views of the world's problems — including those of the United States. Certainly there was national fear since the Great Depression was real. He was deeply concerned at ominous events and happenings here and abroad. In a lengthy editorial for the February 13, 1930, issue, he warned and challenged readers of the paper, asking, "Where Are We Headed?" Some excerpts follow:

"Unless there is a general upheaval in our whole economic system, America's future seems hopeless. Three million married women in the land are now engaged in gainful occupations, which is to say that almost as many married women have given up the glorious privilege of motherhood for money. It means that many men are unable to earn enough by the sweat of their brows and the works of their heads to enable them to support modern American women in the 'style' they demand."

He reasoned that, "Within another decade ... there will be no such thing as individual initiative in the sphere of industry and trade." He pointed out that "Capital has formed giant combines making it the more difficult for the individual man to find employment. ... Parents are selling their little farm homes all across the Southland and moving their families into the industrial centers where they sell their women and even children to the factories for the pitiable sum of five to twelve dollars per week. ... Into this new life the modern fools are pouring their stream of propaganda in support of communism, companionate marriage and even rank Bolshevism, and all social restraints break down. ... One shudders at the thought of what the future will bring."

Freeman envisioned 15 million American men "beginning to stalk along through life with no hope for better days." He was particularly concerned about effects of the depression, communist agitators, possibilities of sabotage, and eventual war.

He had an answer: "The only antidote for the poison now being injected into the veins of our nation is the Gospel of Christ. ... When the day of chaos comes in our land, Christ will be standing on the hill with outstretched hands, crying, 'O, America, America, how oft would I have gathered you, as a hen does her chicks under her wing, and you would not.' And when the awful hate has spent itself and ruin lies all about, Jesus will be standing at our doors, calling us to Himself.

"Collapse in our economic system is certain, but out of the collapse Jesus Christ will get honor for, in the final test, 350,000 evangelicals will be purged and find their souls."

Though the World War II was a decade away, Freeman was on the right track with his concerns.

Bits of Biography, John D. Freeman — Native of Alleene, Arkansas, born February 25, 1884; graduated University of Arkansas, Trinity College (N.C.), and Th.M. from Southern Baptist Theological Seminary; married to Landis Barton; two daughters; served as missionary in Ozarks, pastor of First Church, Springfield, Kentucky, and Belmont Heights Baptist Church, Nashville, Tennessee; named editor of *B&R* while at Belmont Heights; editor of *B&R* 1925-33 until named executive secretary TBC, July 1, 1933; in 1938 led in creating Tennessee Baptist Foundation; resigned 1942 to become editor of *Western Recorder,* Kentucky;died 1974.

CHAPTER SEVEN

Depression and More Wars
Oury Wilburn Taylor
1933-50

Oury W. Taylor had much in common with John D. Freeman, his predecessor. After Editor Freeman's election in 1933 as executive secretary, the helm of the *Baptist and Reflector* needed a new pilot. Freeman had served the paper since 1925, and had witnessed worldwide depression with armed conflict on the horizon.

In addition to editing the paper during World War II, Oury W. Taylor saw the nation work its way out of the hard times of the Depression. He also was on the job when the Korean War broke out.

Pastor of Halls Baptist Church, Tennessee, Taylor was elected by committee, and began serving on July 1, the same day of Freeman's resignation.

Taylor was a native of Kentucky. He was the only son of his father by a second marriage. He was four when his father died, so his childhood prepared him for hard work, perhaps even the difficulties often faced by an editor.

Two years after his election the *Baptist and Reflector*'s centennial year arrived. Editor Taylor honored the Centennial with a sixty-four-page edition of the paper. The paper included many advertisements complimenting the paper as the primary news organ for Tennessee Baptists. He used short biographical information of former editors, along with their photographs.

On the editorial page, he introduced the Centennial to readers:

"The century-old *Baptist and Reflector* celebrates in this issue its one hundred years of service to our people. It reverently pays tribute to the honored dead who in other days guided it through stress and storm and keyed it to the Word of God and the faith of our people revealed there."

He thanked readers of the past, workers of the present, and those who had a loyal history of support for the paper.

He added, "With a hundred years of throbbing history back of it, *Baptist and Reflector* comes to greet our Baptist people and all the people of God everywhere."

In a personal editorial for that special edition Taylor stated his feelings about the century of service:

"Glancing through the yellowing files of this venerable paper stretching back through the years, it is seen that there are certain problems confronting our people now which have confronted Baptists through the century. The circumstances and outward expressions have been different perhaps, but the problems have been the same in essence.

"One sees that, not withstanding disagreement on certain matters, the Word of God and the faith of our people have as a whole been exalted, proclaimed, and lived. However, we feel that the doctrinal distinctiveness and vigor of other days could be recaptured by some of our people today to a distinct advantage.

"Space does not permit nor is it the place here to detail the various controversies among our brethren in other days and the bitterness which was sometimes engendered. We shall let those rest with the past and with the ashes of the honored dead. In that Realm where our brethren have gone on they see eye to eye and all bitterness has vanished."

Not only did Taylor include a short history of the *Baptist and Reflector*, there was a copy of the first page of R.B.C. Howell's *THE BAPTIST* on the front. In addition, he used excerpts from Howell's memorial, which was written while he was in a Nashville prison a short time during the Civil War. It was a story about the first efforts to form a Baptist convention in 1833.

Taylor, like other editors, was bold in expressing his ideas of the paper's role in Tennessee Baptist life. In fact he didn't mind accusations that his paper was heavy in doctrine. In a message less than a month before Japan attacked Pearl Harbor and World War II began, he said, "It stands for the evangelical, cross-centered, Spirit-powered concept and interpretation of the kingdom of God versus the rationalized socialistic concept and interpretation. It gives a Christian interpretation to current events, an interpretation in the light of Scripture, versus the intellectual interpretation whose standards are simply science, philosophy, and psychology."

His boldness can be best expressed in his belief as a December 1940 issue of the paper gave evidence to support his claim that Tennessee Baptist Convention agencies were not immune to constructive criticism.

Much was said and written about war in the years preceding World War II. Tennessee Baptists, in reports, spoke against involvement. As late as 1939, one report read, "… Blood stains of the last world war have not yet dried upon the soils of the nations … ." Taylor seemed to speak for many Tennesseans, vowing support for England, but disavowing military involvement.

War did come, however, and most of the world suffered terribly. The Taylor family lost a son in the Normandy invasion on the French coast. Another son was in the military also.

In the midst of the dark days of world conflict, Taylor several times tackled the question of justifiable war. In the March 4, 1943, issue of the *B&R*, he devoted a page and a half to the subject. He had five parts to the lengthy editorial — Is War Justifiable?, God Taught David to Fight, God and War, Jesus and War, The Conclusion of the Whole Matter.

In his conclusion, he summed up his opinion —

"War is to be avoided as long as possible consistent with justice and honor. When war is thrust upon people, they do not do wrong to wage it.

"We are unalterably opposed to war as a policy and as a program of aggression. But we do not believe the Scriptures sanction the principle of peace at any price.

"We would remove the cause and stop the present war this very minute, if we had the power. But unregenerate nature is still in the world.

"We are conscientiously opposed to epidemics, but believe in fighting them. We are conscientiously opposed to war as a policy, but when it comes, fight through.

"Our nation is far from perfect. But fundamentally it stands for the right in the present conflict. We are fed up with those who constantly lampoon our country for being in the war. Our country did not seek war. War came to it.

"The spirit of the Revolutionary fathers is still in order: 'We pledge our lives, our fortunes, and our sacred honor.' "

There was a report on a meeting of state secretaries (executive directors) in Atlanta, in the January 1, 1942 issue. Called by the Home Mission Board, resolutions concerned ways to support the Armed Forces. An offering throughout the Southern Baptist Convention was agreed upon. The HMB was to use a portion for "work inside the Army camps, and in weak, needy states. Tennessee will use its part for work in Camp Forrest and the industrial areas of our state ... ."

In that same issue an advertisement promoted the plan. "Are Tennessee Baptists interested in salvation of soldiers?" it asked. "What shall we do to help win the soldiers to Christ, help to hold firm those of their number who are already Christians and thus to prepare them the better for the battles that are inevitably before them?" The plan was to share Christ with them in work and training areas before they were moved into battle.

In other matters discussed by Oury Taylor editorially, here are some excerpts:

Patriotism and silence, 1943 — It is often said that patriotism demands that no one criticize the government in wartime lest the war effort be hindered. But this matter has two angles. If by speaking one gives away military secrets and thus gives aid to the enemy and thereby hinders the war effort, then patriotism demands that he keep silent.

But patriotism does not demand that the government not be criticized when it is lax along moral lines. The government's attitude toward liquor traffic, prolific in breeding immorality and crime, silly purchase of dice by military authorities for the morale (?) of soldiers, the governmental insistence of plenty of liquor at the International Food Conference and so on are matters which should be criticized until the criticism burns.

Liquor and military men, 1942 — It is a matter of general knowledge that alcoholism was a major factor in the downfall of

France (World War II). French soldiers could not stand up against Hitler's non-alcoholic soldiers. There are rumors which persist that drinking had something to do with the Pearl Harbor tragedy.

With enemies on both sides, America is probably facing the most critical period in her history as a nation. Soaked soldiers cannot stand up against sober soldiers. Not all Uncle Sam's soldiers are drinkers by any means. … Let America straighten up in order that she may the more quickly stand up against her foes, and please God, overcome them.

Revisiting war, 1942 — *Baptist and Reflector* remembers distinctly how certain men said prior to World War I that mankind was becoming too educated and civilized to resort again to war. One man spent two years preparing a lecture on world peace. Then the war came and spoiled the conclusion of wishful doctrinaires and kept the man from delivering his lecture. Then after the war ended idealists … said this was the end of wars. … If this means they really want peace, let them get right with God in conformity with the Word of God.

Efforts to overthrow Christianity, 1942 — Not long ago *Baptist and Reflector* carried an editorial referring to a pamphlet of the Nazi National German Church being distributed in Germany, in which it was proposed to displace the likeness of the cross in chapels and churches and elsewhere by the swastika. A further quotation reported from the pamphlet … expresses the determination to "extirpate [to pull up by the roots] by all possible methods the Christian faith introduced into Germany 'in the year of disgrace 800' and imposed on the German people, to whose nature and essential being it is entirely alien.

"In the mercy of God there will … come a time which will fulfill a statement by our President that Hitler would discover that 'there is not enough room in the world for God and Hitler.' And Hitler and Hirohito and others of their kind are the ones who shall step down and out, not God!"

[Editor's note: The original editorial January 1, 1942 quoted the pamphlet of the German National Reich Church as follows: On the day the National Church is established, Christ's Cross must be removed from all cathedrals, churches, and chapels within Germany's colonial frontiers. The Cross must be replaced by the sole invincible symbol of Germany — the swastika.]

Front page August 29,1935, taken from History of the Dutch Reformed Church — ... the Baptists may be considered the only Christian Community which has stood since the days of the Apostles, and as a Christian society which has preserved pure the doctrines of the Gospel through all ages. The perfectly correct external and internal economy of the Baptist denomination tends to confirm the truth ... that the Reformation brought about in the sixteenth century was in the highest degree necessary, and at the same time goes to refute the erroneous notion of the Catholics, that their denomination is the most ancient.

The President's message on the Bible, 1935 — The four hundredth anniversary of the printing of the first English Bible is an event of great significance. It challenges the reverent attention of English-speaking peoples the world over. To that day, October 4, when Myles Coverdale, an Augustinian friar, later the bishop of Exeter, produced this book in the common vernacular, we trace a measurable increase not only in the cultural value and influence of this greatest of books, but a quickening in the widespread dissemination of those moral and spiritual precepts that have so greatly affected the progress of Christian civilization. ... We cannot read the history of our rise and development as a nation without reckoning the place the Bible has occupied in shaping the advances of the Republic. ... Its refining and elevating influence is indispensable to our most cherished hopes and ideals (Franklin D. Roosevelt).

American Neutrality, 1935 — One is more and more thankful for the policy of neutrality pursued by the United States government relative to the Italian-Ethiopian conflict. A situation might be conceived whose proximity and circumstances might call for American participation in a war between other parties. But the present situation is not of that kind. The advice of Washington against entangling alliances abroad is still sound. And America would be far better off today if this advice had been heeded in reference to the World War (I). ... If those who call for and bring on war for the sake of profits had to do the sacrificing or the fighting when war came, one is pretty sure that profits would quickly lose their glamour.

A wet paper makes a dry prediction, 1935 — The Social Service Commission of the Southern Baptist Convention reproduces a significant editorial from the Norfolk Ledger-Dispatch of October 16,

1939. In a column entitled "Looking Backward" subtitled "Forty Years Ago" a police action from the past was reported — "Major Charles Kizer, chief of police, instructed members of the police force to arrest all women found in public bar-rooms." The column pointed out that, with superficial differences, "all the rest of the old style characteristics of the public bar-room exist in unnumbered drinking places, licensed drinking places today." There are two characteristics now which would not have tolerated in the old days. First, women are on the same footing on which men are. Second, women, girls, serve the beer and wine in many places. When the issue of prohibition versus legalization comes up for settlement

Oury Wilburn Taylor

again locally or nationally, ought not the voters to go to the polls and vote dry? Legal dryness is the better way to cope with lawless wetness!

The Old Rugged Cross boycotted — It is reported that beginning January 1, 1941, "The Old Rugged Cross" and a long list of other gospel songs, hymns, spirituals, and so on will be boycotted by the radio chains of the country.

The reason appears to be commercial. The songs and music numbers on the blacklist are composers who belong to the American Society of Composers, Authors, and Publishers. The radio chains are unwilling to pay the fee asked for the use of these and will use only the music under their control or numbers over fifty-six years old, which can be used free.

While the radio chains for commercial reasons may boycott "The Old Rugged Cross," millions of other people boycott it for different reasons and in different ways. Many who profess to be devoted to the cross boycott the cross about which they sing. The song may be sung, but the teaching is taboo. Those who reject the substitutionary atonement work of Christ on the cross boycott the cross. All who reject the redemption which is in Christ Jesus boycott the cross. This includes all unbelievers. ... Professed Christians who decline to live sacrificial lives boycott the cross in service, even if they do not boycott it in salvation.

Are these things trivial? — So-called liberals in religion interpret baptism and the Lord's Supper as non-essentials or little things or even trifles. Some frankly say that they are not interested in such. But for a man to disregard the New Testament and propose to measure the value of the ordinances by himself only raises the question of veracity between him and Christ and Paul and others who spoke or wrote on such matters.

Jesus in setting the example for believers when He was baptized, said, "... thus it becomes us to fulfill all righteousness." The example and instruction of Jesus speak the importance of the ordinance for all who wish to follow in His footsteps. At the institution of the Lord's Supper, Jesus said, "This do in remembrance of me." Like baptism, the Supper is clearly and positively enjoined by the Lord. Love should prompt obedience to both.

Oury W. Taylor, *Baptist and Reflector* editor for seventeen years, is recognized as one of Tennessee Baptist's finest leaders. Like all other editors, he dealt with events, such as wars, which intruded on his duties as editor. He had a strong theological focus in his work. He was a valuable partner with John D. Freeman, executive secretary, 1933-42. Since he followed Freeman as *B&R* editor, they knew how to cooperate in Baptist life.

When World War II ended, Taylor devoted the August 25, 1945, front page to all four verses of "The Star-Spangled Banner." He titled his main editorial, "Victory! Hallelujah!" He wrote, "Tuesday, August 14, 1945, was a great day in world history. On that day it was officially announced that Japan had surrendered to the Allies. [Editor's note: Germany and its few European friends already had capitulated]. Praise God, from whom all blessings flow.

"War is a fearful thing. But so is a major operation on a human being. Yet the surgeon's knife is used for the good future effect that is intended. The body politic of the world sometimes requires a major operation. War wields the surgeon's knife. The world could not have peace with Nazi Germany, Fascist Italy, and Imperialistic Japan. ... They had to be whipped and conquered, and they have been. But the joy that attends the result is tempered by the solemn and serious realization that it took a devastating world war to accomplish it and by the solemn and serious realization of the post-war problems to be faced. ... Above all things, let this truth be remembered: Blessed is the nation whose God is the Lord."

In his last editorial, Taylor told of his love for the Convention, the paper, the people he had worked with, and Tennessee Baptists, "Tennessee Baptists are acquainted with the writing I have tried to do. They know about the growth and ministry of the paper. ... But I do want to thank Tennessee Baptists who have let me serve them these years and have faithfully encouraged and supported me and have so leniently judged me. God ever bless and guide you."

The TBC Executive Board published Taylor's *Early Tennessee Baptists* in 1957. He was unable to complete two more Tennessee Baptist volumes, which had been planned.

B its of Biography, Oury W. Taylor — Native of Calloway County, Kentucky; born September 11, 1885; graduated Halls-Moody Institute, McKenzie, and also taught there; graduated from Union University with DD; after being ordained by his home church, was pastor of Trenton, Franklin, Bolivar churches, in Tennessee, and was with Halls Church when he was called to the *B&R;* married to Virgie Glover, and they had two sons. The younger son was killed in action, WW II.

CHAPTER EIGHT

Making Peace
Richard N. Owen
1950-68

In September 1950 Richard Newton Owen was chosen to edit the *Baptist and Reflector* when Oury W. Taylor retired. He served eighteen years, one year longer than Taylor. Though he was not a journalist, he seemed a good fit since he had been pastor of churches in all three Grand Divisions of the state, and had served First Baptist Church, Clarksville, for twelve years. During World War II while he was the Clarksville pastor, the church established a social center for servicemen. He was president of the Tennessee Baptist Convention in 1947.

[Editor's note: The *B&R* has had three editors with journalism experience — Shackleford, Allen, and Wilkey, all professional journalists; Lester also had some experience.]

Owen's newspaper ministry began as the paper continued to face severe financial trouble. In January 1949, the paper got its own printing facility. Severe financial problems forced the Convention to purchase printing equipment in order to continue publishing. The TBC executive board formed Tennessee Baptist Press, Inc. after several months of study and negotiating for a printing contract. TBP printed the paper from then through January 1978 — when commercial printing costs were lower because of innovations, such as offset printing.

Edwin E. Deusner, president of TBP, explained in the *B&R* (January 6, 1949) that *"Baptist and Reflector* has never sought to make money. Its whole purpose was to give the Baptists of Tennessee in particular and Southern Baptists in general a sound, constructive, informative journal. Financially speaking, its only hope was to break even, and we were successful in this for a number of years... ."

In 1960 the TBC terminated TBP and placed the production

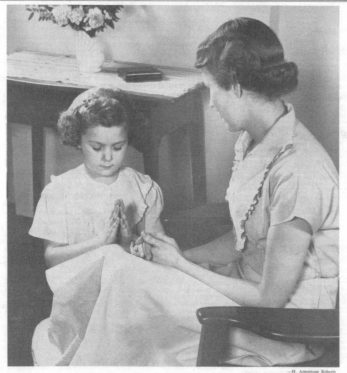

BAPTIST &
REFLECTOR

JOURNAL OF
TENNESSEE BAPTIST
CONVENTION

"SPEAKING THE TRUTH IN LOVE"

VOLUME 123   NUMBER 11   THURSDAY, MARCH 14, 1957

Learning Life's Greatest Lesson At Mother's Knee

The cover of the March 14, 1957 issue of the Baptist and Reflector.

under the Executive Board's administrative committee. The committee was told to "develop policies for, and direct the editor in, the management of the *Baptist and Reflector*, safeguarding the editorial freedom of the editor."

Albert Wardin refers to Convention minutes of 1960 and notes that "... even with the ideal of a free press, Tennessee Baptists lost

at this time the opportunity to place the paper under a separate board of trustees, nominated by the Convention, such as Kentucky, Virginia, and Texas." The idea of a separate board for the paper was discussed at length by the executive committee and D.L. Lowrie when he was executive director, with favorable agreement but no action was ever taken.

We see then, that publishing a denominational paper requires sound financial support, as well as responsible and creative leadership. Sufficient funding is vital so that the paper can fill its role within the Convention family.

Richard N. Owen

Editorially Owen opposed Baptist entities accepting federal loans for construction or any other cause. He also opposed court rulings prohibiting prayer and Bible reading in public schools, saying, "We cannot see why voluntary prayer and Bible reading should be forbidden in any school." He also expressed his feeling that an amendment to the Constitution might be needed to permit these expressions. He believed safeguards to free exercise of religion should be enacted. And he stood against the idea that any government could mandate any religious observance, be it required prayer or Bible reading.

Owen's first paper was published September 21, 1950. As is the usual case in leadership changes, he thanked his predecessor: "Dr. Taylor has rendered a great service to our people in his staunch and untiring defense of the faith once and for all delivered unto the saints. He has labored long and well as an able and sound exponent of conservative theology and is held in respect far and wide as such... . "

Editor Owen wrote to his readers: "Your new editor comes to the *Baptist and Reflector* with the feeling that a very heavy and challenging responsibility and opportunity has been committed to him by his brethren … ."

The entire editorial page was devoted to the change at the helm. He included a spiritual daily prayer and pledge to serve well with God's help, which he invoked. And he greeted his subscribers with a welcome formed as a poem, closing with this verse (in paragraph form here): "The *Baptist and Reflector* has been and will be a Baptist paper with an unashamed faith reflecting the light of our times in the light of the timeless. Through it you should declare yourselves; for the Lord's people dare not be dumb when truth must be expressed in word uttered or written."

During Richard Owen's years as editor, the paper carried much TBC departmental news, week by week. Each department (or group) had its own logo as a heading. Some issues were largely promotional, even to printing Sunday School and Training Union attendance figures weekly at all reporting churches. Bellevue, Memphis, usually was near the top. For example, a September 28, 1950 listing reported Bellevue with 2,585 for Sunday School and 1,044 in Training Union. Highland Park, Chattanooga, reported 3,527 in Sunday School.

Some excerpts from Owen's editorials and opinion pieces:

Integrity, 1950 — We are no stronger nationally than the fiber of the character of our citizenship. Ancient China knew no protection from the enemy without though she stretched a stone curtain all along her northern border in the form of the Great Wall of China. She had in the long run only the security that was hers in gate-keepers who had integrity that was unbribeable. Where a gatekeeper could be bought, she had no more security than if the wall had not existed. In fact she had less, because in forgetting human weakness she had depended on what of itself can never be sufficient for protection.

We have no security in the long run beyond integrity in all those who hold the gateways of our defenses. It is utter folly to put our hope in mere physical means to protect. It is time for us to open our eyes to just what can be counted on in this hour.

Interview with Toyohiko Kagawa, Japanese Christian apologist, 1950 — Kagawa, a cabinet member in post-war (WW II) Japan, had traveled widely in the United States. Owen interviewed him after

Kagawa spoke in Nashville. Owen asked him of his opinion on another world war. His answer: "Chinese communists say it has already started. I say it is avoidable. You Christians can help. Japan must be converted. ... You have in America two extremes: heaven people and hell people. Among you I have experienced the best people in the world. If that power could just be harnessed. Tennessee is known in Japan. You need a TVA for Christian power." Earlier Kagawa had said in his message, "There are still millions who cannot understand Jesus. Jesus thought about God. He spent nights praying for the remaking of mankind. ... It is absolutely necessary to be awakened to the need for love. Help us to repent, O God!"

The knowledge we need, 1959 — How much of our brain do we use? The mechanism of memory in the brain provides a vast filing system. ... Einstein's theory of relativity and Max Planck's quantum theory have had their impact on what we think we know about the universe. ... Shots are now being taken at the moon. ... There is a lot of talk about man making a space trip. ... We should be pretty skeptical about all of this. A trip even to the moon, the nearest thing to earth, presents an enormous series of difficulties. ... We are creatures of this habitable earth. The moon, of course, is dead.

The only planet in our solar system which might possibly support life is Mars. ... This is simply written down in view of some of the absurdities that are now being said concerning space travel as if it were near at hand. Our desperately needed knowledge is not how to reach other planets, or the moon, as conquerors of space. Our urgent problem is humbly learning to become children of God. It lies in accepting His plan by which we can live together in faith, hope, and love while here on this earth. ... Above all, we need a true knowledge of God.

Being part-time Christians, 1959 — Recently a prominent missions leader in West Germany said that Christianity might lose the race among the world's great religions unless it fully recognized its missionary task ... that Christianity must succeed in arousing individual Christians to help fulfill its role. This task is winning the lost. ... Christianity fails as it becomes professionalized religion depending altogether on those who are paid to fulfill the role of witness and soul winner.

Liquor and cigarettes, 1959 — Cigarettes and liquor manufacturers have been fighting for a long time to end their tax stamps.

Now they have won. Your government will take the loss. Other taxpayers will eventually have to absorb this loss. ... The cigarette and liquor industries are riding high. The liquor industry also got its price hike assured in Tennessee in our last legislature. This parasitical business manages to get many favors for itself. All the while it keeps destroying homes and damning lives.

God and the public school, 1959 — We agree ... that American schools need to teach more about God than ever before. The early teaching of our country had spiritual and moral content which is lacking today. ... The principle of free public education and church-state separation must be upheld. But the fact that this is a cherished principle ought in no wise allow a climate unfriendly to religion to prevail in our public school system. ... Tax money cannot be used directly or indirectly for the support of schools operated under church control. This, our traditional American belief, must not be sacrificed.

Political and national loyalties, 1959 — The question of political and national loyalties keeps being raised since some of those being mentioned prominently as candidates for president and vice president of the United States are adherents of the Roman Catholic faith. Under our form of government in America, no religious qualification is made a test for public office. ... None of us as Americans can oppose any candidate on the basis of his religious adherence. But ... we can very well exercise our franchise and elect ... those about whom there will be no possible question as to their loyalty and devotion to the United States of America.

Proclamation and witness, 1966 — Entering 1966 we face obstacles and hindrances to the Gospel's progress. Successive crises confront us with a seeming unending state of emergency. Western civilization to an alarming degree has lost its faith. World conditions appear less favorable to Christianity. Virulent communism, strident nationalism, corrosive secularism, wars both cold and hot, resurgent non-Christian religions, imprisoned Christian missionaries, refugees by thousands fleeing their homeland — all these and other evidences of rebellion and revolution tempt us to conclude, Our world isn't ready for the Gospel. Perhaps we hope the Lord will exempt us from the duty to proclaim the Gospel and witness to Christ.

But we should learn from the first century. What they did was not under favorable circumstances. The Gospel actually made its advances in the midst of most unlikely conditions. Whatever doors the first disciples found opened were accompanied by adversaries. ... Proclamation and witness are essential to the church's life. ...

BAPTIST & REFLECTOR

JOURNAL OF
TENNESSEE BAPTIST CONVENTION

"SPEAKING THE TRUTH IN LOVE"
VOLUME 12? NUMBER 14 THURSDAY, APRIL 4, 1957

The COOPERATIVE PROGRAM

A Helping Hand to a Needy World
Tennessee Baptist Goal for 1957 — $2,800,000
Southern Baptist Goal for 1957 — $11,000,000

The cover of the April 4, 1957 issue of the Baptist and Reflector.

Our objective must always be to proclaim the Gospel so as to win souls to Christ and to grow New Testament churches.

Your child and television, 1966 — We can't dismiss television. It will stay. But we dare not be indifferent to what it is presenting, particularly to children. In many respects it is determining their future. They have not yet learned to determine themselves to evaluate what they see and hear, nor to reject what is cheap, shoddy, and repulsive. ... Do we speak out against "sick" humor? Do we condemn the television fare constantly piped into our living rooms which cancerously attack the basic social attitudes providing the foundation for civilized human relations?

By the mid-1960s, the *Baptist and Reflector* had a new cover design and redesigned inside layout. An attractive photograph — portraying people of all ages and circumstances usually covered the front page each week.

Richard Owen, having served as editor for eighteen years, announced his retirement in the April 18, 1968 issue. A new editor would be installed in September. He had seen discord, growth, war circumstances, and changes within the Tennessee Baptist Convention and also with the Southern Baptist Convention.

T.B. Maston, then retired professor of Christian Ethics at Southwestern Baptist Theological Seminary, wrote a series of essays on the Christian life — for State Baptist newspapers. The first article depicted "Tendencies that Threaten the SBC." The article endeavored to answer some baffling questions. No doubt editors appreciated the help!

Owen used Maston's essay in April 1968. In it, Maston pointed to five tendencies that faced Southern Baptists. One was of particular interest to Owen and other Baptist editors. Maston said, "There seems to be a tendency toward a controlled press. This may be an accomplished fact rather than a tendency. It is potentially extremely dangerous. State denominational papers are owned and controlled by state conventions. They evidently cannot live without convention support.

"We should help the editors ... to maintain as much independence as possible. This should include resistance to efforts in some states for the papers to be controlled directly by the executive committee or board of the state. We should be grateful for courageous editors who speak as prophets of God through the pages of their papers. Let us not forget that a controlled press by a state convention or by an agency of the Southern Baptist Convention is a threat to our churches and our denomination."

The committee, which was to nominate his successor, asked Owen to describe "what an editor ought to be." He responded editorially with a "profile" in the April 18 issue — educationally prepared, especially in English and journalism; intellectually alert, spiritually motivated, biblically grounded, experienced in local convention's life, a writer who can use the English language with precision, directness, clarity, simplicity, honest; a man who can stand pressure, a man who can devote himself to his editorial task wholeheartedly. And he elaborated on these and other positive points.

He told the committee that the profile "is not my own likeness to be sure."

Bits of Biography, Richard Newton Owen — Native of Covington, Tennessee; born April 1, 1898; educated at Tulane University, New Orleans, and University of Tennessee, Knoxville; ThM. degree, Southern Baptist Theological Seminary, Louisville, Kentucky; honorary DD., Union University; pastor of First Baptist Church, Milan; First Baptist Church, Elizabethton; First Baptist Church, Paris; and First Baptist Church, Clarksville, all in Tennessee; married to Margaret McNairy Steele; one son, Richard Jr.; wide range of service with Tennessee Baptist Convention and Southern Baptist Convention.

CHAPTER NINE

Transitions, First Woman Editor

James A. Lester
1968-73
Eura Lannom
1974-76

Richard N. Owen announced his retirement in April 1968, and served through that September. A successor was selected and James A. Lester took office with the first October issue. Transition and change were in order — Owen had edited the paper for eighteen years. He had built subscriptions to the highest number ever. Lester spent several weeks in orientation and getting acquainted with Tennessee Baptists.

Lester had a long career in promotion and public relations, and had served as pastor with churches in Georgia, Mississippi, and Louisiana. He was a photographer and also had taught school. Owen introduced Lester in his last issue, September 26.

The new editor came to the *Baptist and Reflector* from the Georgia Baptist Convention where he was secretary of promotion and public relations. While editing the *B&R*, he also wrote *A History of the Georgia Baptist Convention 1822-1972,* for which he was under contract.

Lester's first issue of the paper revealed a new design for the pages with a more "open" appearance. A weekly column by Executive Secretary W. Fred Kendall was introduced. More photographs were used. He continued using a column on family life written by B. David Edens of Stephens College, Columbia, Missouri.

Lester spoke to subscribers on the editorial page, "As a stranger in your midst there is an aspect of an unknown quantity. It is my sincere desire and objective to become acquainted personally with you, pastor and people, as quickly as possible. I hope you will allow me this privilege.

"As successor to a distinguished Christian editor and leader as Dr. Richard N. Owen, I come to office with humility and with the prayer that my efforts might be acceptable to you as they are directed to the spiritual and practical tasks before us."

The next issue, October 10, honored the retired Owen with several features. David Keel, *B&R* circulation manager, wrote an article describing Owen's work, a thorough biographical sketch was included, and a guest editorial by Kendall expressed appreciation from Tennessee Baptists. "Pulpit to Pew," a weekly column was introduced, written by Jim Griffith, Georgia pastor, who later became Georgia Baptists' executive secretary.

James A. Lester

In an October 1968 editorial Lester reminded readers of the November national elections. "It was eight years ago that some Southern Baptists were writing and speaking at length and often heatedly concerning the then upcoming presidential election. At issue was the possible election of a Catholic for president. This subject drew a lot of mileage out of typewriter ribbons. Four years ago and again this year, we sensed a lethargy in the minds and hearts of people," he wrote. He confessed that the editorial's purpose was not an endorsement of any candidate.

He added, "It is clearly within the framework of Christian responsibility to encourage an active interest in the affairs of our world, and particularly our nation." He urged readers to be involved at "every level of elective choice to make an impact upon a secular society."

A news story in the October 31 issue told of a position paper from a committee appointed at the June SBC session, concerning "the crisis in the nation." Program leaders, said the story, are proposing actions which will help deal with the causes of national unrest. The crisis study was studied from the standpoint of injustice, disrespect for law, inadequate education and housing, unem-

BAPTIST

AND

REFLECTOR

VOL. 135 / THURSDAY, OCTOBER 2, 1969 / NO. 40

NEWS-JOURNAL OF THE TENNESSEE BAPTIST CONVENTION

Open House - - New Baptist Building
- - And they came from everywhere.

The October 2, 1969, issue features the Open House in the New Baptist Building in Brentwood.

ployment, poverty, limitations of citizenship rights, mass media, weak family life, rebellion toward God, racial prejudice, paternalism, racial segregation, selective evangelism, lack of communication, lack of vital Christian faith, and an inadequate communication of the gospel to the lost people.

During Lester's tenure America's efforts to explore outer space proved successful. Just ten years earlier, *B&R* Editor Richard Owen had written of the space program, "We should be pretty skeptical about all of this."

Said Lester, "A world waited, many prayed, and during the last days of 1968, one of history's greatest news stories was written — the flight of Apollo 8! The greatest news story is, of course, the story of the birth of our Savior. In secular events, the moon voyage must surely rank high. Of significance is the tremendous spiritual impact of the reading of the creation story from Genesis 1:1 by the astronauts as they hurtled through space some 235,000 miles from earth.

"In a day of rebellion, unrest, and war, this is a significant statement. ... The recognition of Jehovah God as creator of the universe by those who would explore this universe is the first prerequisite for successful space flight." He acknowledged the bravery of Frank Borman, James S. Lovell Jr., and William Anders, and commented that this flight was not the end of space exploration.

He was right about flights to outer space. In July the following year, America landed a space ship on the moon, and astronaut Neil Armstrong announced to the world, "The Eagle has landed," as he stepped onto the moon's surface. In his July 24 editorial, Lester applauded the event — and Armstrong, Buzz Aldrin, and Michael Collins. "We thank God for this tremendous scientific step forward," he wrote, "We predict that man will eventually live in colonies on the moon, and in due season as it must be for that which is worth obtaining, man will explore and inhabit yet other planets even more distant than the moon."

About this time Tennessee legislators began making noise in a push to allow pari-mutuel betting on horse and dog racing. Lester immediately voiced opposition on the part of Tennessee Baptists. On the front of the March 20, 1969, issue, he alerted his constituency for action, "This is an urgent plea to Tennessee Baptists for action now in a situation where our response, or our silence, will identify us for a long time to come. ... Documented studies of gambling are numerous. Conclusions of these studies present a picture which leaves no doubt concerning the numerous evils inherent in the proposal. ... Tennessee Baptists ought to be convinced of the evils ... ." He pointed to the strength of 850,000 Baptist church members, saying many voted when candidates sought public office as a public trust. Lester urged Tennessee Baptist churches and associations to petition the legislators to drop the gambling effort.

When the TBC met in annual session with Broadway Church, Knoxville, in November 1968, the executive board honored Eura Lannom for her twenty-five years of service with the *Baptist and Reflector*, and Richard Owen, the retired editor. Messengers elected Tom Madden, Tullahoma pastor, to the presidency. Six years later Lannom served as acting editor for two years, and Madden was executive director 1979-89. The paper had photos of all three in the Convention report issue.

During late summer of 1969, Convention offices were moved into a new building on the corner of Franklin Pike and Maryland Way in Brentwood. It was the first all-new building designed and built expressly for the Tennessee Baptist Convention. Editor Lester reported on progress during construction, and amplified the stories with photographs.

The Convention met in Nashville that November, so an Open House was planned for the new building in September. Lester welcomed visitors in an editorial, "Difficulties of moving from the Belmont Boulevard location to Brentwood and difficulties in adjustment in the new building have been largely resolved." An editorial partner to that welcome stressed the need for a strong thrust by the churches in Cooperative Program giving. He was a proponent of the CP and supported the plan often on the editorial page.

For the celebration of the new facility, Lester's pre-convention issue was forty pages featuring Convention news and congratulatory notes, and on the cover a likeness of Sinking Creek Baptist Church, the oldest Tennessee Baptist church structure. [He mistakenly claimed that issue to be "the largest paper in its history." When O.W. Taylor produced the November 2, 1935, *B&R* Centennial paper, there were sixty-four pages; John Freeman produced a ninety-two page edition in 1930.]

Some snippets from Lester editorials follow:

A time for prayer, 1972 — Addressing the need for prayer in the selection of a successor to the retiring executive secretary, W. Fred Kendall, he wrote, "Like the pastor of a church, he must be a man of many talents and many abilities. With the confidence of the constituency he must be a leader. He must likewise be an effective and able administrator, a visionary with pragmatic ability, a conciliator, advisor, and many other things to many people. This office is one of the most difficult offices in Christian leadership. ... We believe that when God has a place, He also has a man for that place. ... To this end, Tennessee Baptists must pray, and pray earnestly that these men (seeking a person for the job) will be filled with the Spirit of God, and will know when God speaks."

Thanksgiving for cease-fire, 1973 — Americans as a nation and as individuals had agonized and many have been troubled in conscience and heart over the (Vietnam) war in the first place, and over the loss of American lives ... 45,933 of her finest young men killed, 303,000 wounded. ... We give thanks to God and we give expressions of heartfelt gratitude for the accomplishment of a cease-fire. The undeclared war has created divisiveness, hawks and doves, militants on both sides of thought concerning involvement, and could have damaged severely the unity of this nation.

We pray that this nation might be spared further conflicts and military actions. We are not optimistic, but we can and do pray knowing God still controls the universe, if His creation will be directed by Him.

Keeping the lights on, 1973 — Tennessee and Southern Baptists are placing special emphasis this year on the importance of the Sunday Training Union and evening worship services. This emphasis is much needed and long overdue. ... When the lights have gone out on Sunday evening, much spiritual vitality has gone out of the churches. The Church Training Department has made substantial efforts to put new life into training. ... It is very important that we rethink our posture on our Sunday evening programs. They have blessed us and been a blessing for many, many years. They have a place in Baptist life, and cannot be ignored.

James Lester's leadership with the paper ended with his resignation in 1974. There was a brief notice in the October 18, 1973, issue, from the administrative committee of the Executive Board, granting a six-month leave of absence. The chairman stated that Ralph Norton, executive secretary, would be in charge of the paper.

Lester explained the following week with a personal message. He had been injured in an automobile accident in 1972, he said, and pain from back injuries persisted. Doctors suggested he needed time to rest. Lester resigned at the conclusion of the six-months leave.

Eura Rich Lannom, 1974-76

The two years following James Lester's resignation as *Baptist and Reflector* editor have a unique place in history. Ralph Norton, TBC executive secretary, took charge of the paper for a brief time. But he soon turned to Eura Rich Lannom, and shifted regular operational responsibilities to her.

Thus Lannom was the first *B&R* leader without experience as a pastor. Not only that, she was, and remains, the only woman editor, though she was given title of acting editor, and served for two years. She was a likely choice for the leadership role — she had been on the paper's staff for thirty-one years. And she had worked with three editors, O.W. Taylor, Richard N. Owen, and James A. Lester. [She later served with Alvin Shackleford when Lester resigned.] Also, she had worked with Norton for several months, and would continue to do so. She had knowledge and experience of producing the paper. And though capable, she was a reluctant "editor."

In his book *Tennessee Baptists, a Comprehensive History 1779-1999*, Albert Wardin writes, "Although it was most unique among Southern Baptists for a woman to serve as editor of a state paper, her role was circumscribed in that she was only an acting editor on a temporary assignment without inclination or opportunity to express her own ideas editorially or set editorial policy."

Lannom continued several features initiated by Owen and Lester, i.e., "Pulpit to Pew," "Interpretations" by Herschel Hobbs, Ralph Norton's personal column, and a devotional column written by Tennessee Baptist women and men. Previews of Sunday School lessons also were continued, as well as "Powerline," a weekly feature from the SBC Radio-Television Commission aimed for Baptist youth. [The Commission was dissolved later.]

A series of articles by R. Paul Caudill alerted Tennesseans on the evils of pari-mutuel betting. The January 16, 1975, issue, carried a thorough discussion of early planning for retirement years, written by E. Lee Sizemore. That issue also used guest editorials on ministering to the minister, from the *Maryland Baptist*, and the Cooperative Program, from the *Alabama Baptist*.

Bobbie Durham, staff writer, reported on Convention meetings regularly. For example, she wrote about the 1975 Evangelism Conference featuring Lewis Drummond, Jack Stanton, Carl Bates, Ralph Norton, and others. The report was typical good coverage of Convention ministries.

Durham was fatally injured in an automobile accident while working on January 15, 1981.

February issues featured another guest editorial from Mississippi's *Baptist Record*, an explanatory essay by Herschel Hobbs on the Baptist Faith and Message, and an essay by Albert

Eura Rich Lannom

McClellan, Executive Committee, SBC, staffer. McClellan wrote about the down side of television. "That little black box with the big glass eye is the fire that is generating evil on our own hearths," he wrote. "The rattlesnakes are coming. What on earth are we going to do? ... Don't we see what goes into a child someday will come out?

"Where are our handles? Time is running out for American morality. Surely there are handles. One of them is the knob on your television set. Another is the dollar you refuse to spend on the program sponsors. Another is your angry letter to the stations, the network, and the sponsors. Perhaps the best handle is the simple teaching of God's Word to our own little children. ... Teaching it to youth and adults might help too."

In July 1975, the paper carried a report on Baptist State papers. The report came from a committee appointed in 1974, and chaired by H. Franklin Paschall, pastor of Nashville's First Baptist Church. The report stated, "There is nothing more distinctly Southern Baptist than Baptist State papers. ... As the papers came into being in response to a mighty missionary movement ... they themselves were possessed with a great missionary purpose. ... Our missionary purpose has been well served as these papers have informed, indoctrinated, inspired and unified our people."

When James L. Sullivan, Baptist Sunday School Board president, retired in 1975, Lannom featured him in one of her few editorials. "I remember him as a pastor and have known him as a denominational worker all these twenty-two years," she said. "Achievements made during these years would be impossible to enumerate; but if one had visited in 1952 and should make a return visit today, he might find himself lost in trying to find his way around the mammoth-sized buildings. The buildings and the growth of all the other physical assets are not as important as the integrity of Dr. Sullivan and the faithfulness to perform his task. ... Mrs. Sullivan, we thank you to for sharing your husband with Southern Baptists and give you credit for your share in his success."

She managed the paper, while consulting regularly with Norton. Her knowledge of the daily operation of the paper, the programs and policies of the Tennessee Baptist Convention, and understanding the role of cooperating with the churches, enabled her to keep the paper true to its role.

Alvin C. Shackleford, who was elected editor in September 1976, later noted that, "No one can estimate the number of news items that Eura has written and edited during these forty-two years. Nor can anyone estimate the influence her gracious spirit has had on Tennessee Baptists during this period."

Betty Williams, who has been a *B&R* staff member for forty-six years, remembers Eura Lannom as an effective leader during her tenure, and who relied on Norton and other leaders for advice and suggestions. Williams' years with the paper coincided with Lannom, and she is still on the staff (October 2005).

Lannom's specialty was printing scores of small news items of Tennessee Baptist churches and the people. She also was a strong supporter of the Cooperative Program and missions.

When Shackleford became *Baptist and Reflector* editor in November 1976, he named Eura Lannom assistant to the editor; she retired April 1977. She wrote a personal editorial for the October 28, 1976, issue — a "thank you letter" to Tennessee Baptists, and welcoming Shackleford.

She lauded Tennessee Baptist leadership and church members for support, especially when she served as acting editor. Here are some excerpts:

"Tennessee Baptists, you are a great group of Christians. You were there when I first joined the church, and because of you I am what I have become in my Christian life. You provided what I needed along the way. ... Since February 1, 1943, I have been privileged to serve on the staff of editors O.W. Taylor, Richard N. Owen, and James A. Lester. ... When I was approached about serving as acting editor I refused and cited five reasons for not doing it. I was reminded that I had been asked only to pray and think about it...

"When it was discussed with me again, I felt that it might be that the Lord had prepared me for this interim period which I expected to be only a few months; I would do my best to hold everything together until they (the committee) secured an editor. ... I kept asking the Lord to give me the wisdom, and understanding which came only from knowing him as Lord of my life. I trusted him to direct my path."

Lannom in particular expressed appreciation for the *B&R* staff, pastors and other church leaders, lay persons, and association missionaries. "Remember," she said, "the *Baptist and Reflector* supports all work of the Tennessee Baptist Convention and the Southern Baptist Convention. Brother pastors, you and your church members need the *Baptist and Reflector*."

When she retired, Shackleford acknowledged her value as a long-term staff member. "She has held many titles with your weekly newsjournal," he wrote, "but as this staff is organized she had her talented hand in everything that went into and around the *Baptist and Reflector*. For those who have trouble dealing with one editor, Eura had to put up with four — Taylor, Owen, Lester, and the present editor!

"For all of us it will be hard to think of the *Baptist and Reflector* without thinking of Eura, and to think of Eura Lannom without thinking of the *Baptist and Reflector* — especially on those hectic go-to-press Mondays."

B its of Biography, James A. Lester — Born December 18, 1928, Edison, Georgia; educated Norman Junior College and Mercer University, Georgia; and New Orleans Baptist Theological Seminary,

New Orleans; employed by New Orleans paper, pastor of churches in Georgia, Mississippi, and Louisiana, and other church staff positions; school teacher, photographer; married to Doris Holland, two sons.

Bits of Biography, Eura Rich Lannom — Born at Holland, Kentucky; studied at business college; worked with Training Union Department and other TBC areas; worked at Baptist Book Store in Nashville; began work with *Baptist and Reflector* 1943, served in various capacities until retirement 1976; acting editor of *B&R* 1974-76; married to G.E. Lannom. Died Oct. 16, 1994.

CHAPTER TEN

First in Era of Journalists
Alvin C. Shackleford
1976-87

A the TBC Executive Board meeting in Brentwood, September 21, 1976, Alvin C. Shackleford was elected editor of the *Baptist and Reflector*. He had spent eleven years at the helm of the *Indiana Baptist*. The Indiana paper was much smaller in subscription numbers but it was a valuable school for the new editor, offering experience in Baptist life at the state and national levels.

Shackleford's employment brought a new look and better understanding of the paper's role among Tennessee Baptists. He was a trained and experienced journalist, the first for the *B&R*. The Georgia native earned a BA degree in journalism from the University of Georgia, and an MDiv. degree from Southwestern Baptist Theological Seminary.

Journalism education and hands-on experience helped Shackleford in his new office. For the first time in its history, writing and editing skills, plus on the job experience, would enhance an already durable and recognizable Tennessee Baptist newsjournal. Previous editors had depended on desire and hard work to produce a viable paper worthy of its goal. Shackleford proved to be well qualified for the position, even though controversy and conflict swirled about the Convention and elsewhere during his tenure.

An article in Shackleford's second issue, November 11, 1976, touched on religion and politics. A Baptist Press story reviewed voting in the election of Jimmy Carter, a Southern Baptist, as president of the United States. In an interview, James L. Sullivan, retired BSSB president and then current SBC president, said the election offered American people "a wonderful option to high grade men (Carter and Gerald Ford)."

Sullivan said Carter's candidacy had brought the SBC to the attention of large numbers of the news media in the East, "who had no idea of what or who Southern Baptists are."

"I hope Carter can be an influence for religious liberty around the world in his handling of international affairs of America," he added. "As we become a larger denomination, it is inevitable by the law of averages we will have more Baptists in places of leadership. We teach our people to be Christian citizens."

The new editor in his first editorials written for November 18, 1976 discussed guidelines for letters and the purpose of a Baptist State paper. E.C. Routh, a retired Oklahoma editor, was the writer. Shackleford also told readers that he was bringing "Cicero's Comment" with him to the new job. The column was like a personal letter to the readers, and he explained that Cicero was his father's middle name and his also. Cicero quickly became a well-liked item, with wry humor, and Shackleford's deft use of clever names for quaint church members and pastors. He also invited Tom Madden, TBC executive secretary, to write a weekly column.

Routh's guidelines included information, instruction, inspiration, enlistment, and, unification. Shackleford's letters page was lively and often dealt with controversy. The letters page became an open forum and sounding board. His rules — letter writers must relate to interests of Tennessee Baptists and other Christians, deal with issues rather than persons, be brief, sign your letter, copies of letters will not be used.

Shackleford's tenure spanned uneasy years in Southern Baptist life. Often those years introduced controversy, which spilled over into Tennessee Baptist affairs. During his editorship the SBC move toward conservatism began. Editing a Baptist State paper became a more tenuous and sometimes perilous position.

During the year now remembered as the real beginning of conservative resurgency, Shackleford initiated improvements in publication. In a move for economy and efficiency that provided more space for the paper, Shackleford introduced a new format in the first issue of 1979. Pages of the *B&R* had been printed tabloid size for a century. That size was most efficient and economical at that time, and could have been the only size available because of printing press standard sizes. For several years prior to Shackleford's tenure, magazine size was used.

When Shackleford changed the page size to tabloid, most readers approved. Tabloid remained the preferred size through subsequent years, and for the same reasons. He explained to readers, "The new printing and addressing processes are decidedly faster than those previously used. This means that each issue will contain more current news — and that many people in the state will receive the *Baptist and Reflector* one day earlier each week." He assured readers that ... "one thing will not change — our desire to present to you each week the best possible state paper for the Baptists of Tennessee."

In April 1979 an ongoing situation within the Tennessee Baptist Convention finally was resolved. Action was taken by messengers to a called Convention session, the first such meeting in 104 years. It dealt with Belmont Plaza, a Nashville property owned by the TBC.

Alvin C. Shackleford

Evidently, the property, intended for retirees housing, was a financial problem.

Editor Shackleford had used many pages of the paper in previous weeks thoroughly discussing and explaining every aspect of the situation. The called session on April 11 drew 1,396 messengers — who settled the issue at the end of the day with a vote to sell Belmont Plaza.

Shackleford's report said, "In a special called session of the Tennessee Baptist Convention, the messengers approved a motion that Belmont Plaza, a 123-unit apartment building for senior adults, be sold or transferred 'to relieve the Tennessee Baptist Service Corporation as an agency of the Tennessee Baptist Convention from all liability on said lease.' "

He wrapped up the action by declaring editorially, "This is the best possible decision."

He concluded, "The task is not over. The committee (named to act on the decision to sell) ... and the Executive Board still have much work to do. But the messengers met and considered the alternatives, and gave directions for the future of Belmont Plaza." A

Franklin Web, a printing company in Franklin, has printed the Baptist and Reflector *weekly on Monday nights since the editorship of Al Shackleford.*

group of Baptist laypersons and pastors took over the facility in May 1980.

The Belmont Plaza problem dominated TBC life for months before the April 11 meeting. And it required many hours and pages of valuable *B&R* time and space. But the editor responded as a skilled journalist should.

In May 1979, Shackleford's effort to employ another experienced journalist was realized when Charlie Warren was named associate editor. A native of Roanoke, Virginia, Warren was associate editor of *World Mission Journal,* a publication of the then Brotherhood Commission (now dissolved), SBC; and with the then Foreign Mission Board (International Mission Board). He was a graduate of Oklahoma Baptist University and Southwestern Baptist Theological Seminary. He remained on the staff until 1988 when he took the editorship of *Home Life,* a magazine of the BSSB. (Editor's note: As of October 2005 he is editor of the *Arkansas Baptist News.*)

Bringing Warren onto the *B&R* staff enhanced news coverage, feature writing, page makeup and design, and photography. The staff now had two trained and experienced journalists, a bonus for any Baptist State paper.

The second major news event for Tennessee Baptists in 1979 was the beginning of the conservative "take over" in the Southern Baptist Convention. Adrian Rogers, pastor of Bellevue Baptist Church, Memphis, was elected president on the first ballot, over five other candidates — Robert Naylor, William Self, Abner McCall, Douglas Watterson (Knoxville pastor), and C.E. Price. McCall was elected first vice president.

Convention sessions were held in Houston's The Summit, and a Bold Missions Rally in the Astrodome featured evangelist Billy Graham and an audience of more than 48,000 Baptists. (Editor's note: The following week Graham held a crusade in Nashville.)

The paper reported on the front page, "Amid charges and countercharges, messengers also adopted a motion disavowing 'overt political activity and organization as a method of selection of its officers,' " and said that convention messengers took several other actions leading toward the conservative right. According to *B&R* reporting, former TBC pastor and SBC president Wayne Dehoney leveled charges of "overt political activities" at Paul Pressler, a Houston Appellate Court judge.

"Pressler, who helped lead a conservative coalition to elect Rogers president, denied rumors that he and others encouraged local churches to bus messengers to the convention for the election, and that some churches had more than the maximum of ten messengers."

Following that Convention, messengers have continued to elect conservative presidents, often with only one candidate. And leaders of most, if not all, SBC entities, including seminaries, are conservative theologically.

A Baptist Press news feature July 4, 1979, said, "Southern Baptist newspaper editors commenting on the recent annual Southern Baptist Convention in Houston saw it as a bitter-sweet example of Southern Baptists at their worst and best. The best, they said, came in the form of an extravaganza ... as more than 48,000 Southern Baptists and others saw 1,100 missionaries dedicated and another 1,200 volunteer for mission service. ... The worst ... came in the form of unprecedented political maneuvering mixed with allegations of voting irregularities, which took place during suc-

111

cessful efforts to elect a president committed to inerrancy as an issue."

As for Al Shackleford's interpretation of the Convention's actions and outcome, he wrote in his editorial that words were inadequate. "We ran the complete gamut from the exhilarating excitement of the Wednesday night Astrodome service to charges of despicable political activity. ... The divisive spirit seemed to begin at the Sunday night Pastor's Conference, which at times took on an atmosphere more of a political rally than a worship service. ... If all these things (accusations) were true, and apparently they are to some extent, it is a disgraceful display of methods and motives which have no place in our denomination."

Commenting on the newly elected president, Shackleford wrote, "Our new president has made a tremendous beginning. Not only has he said he wanted to be open, positive, and transparent, but he demonstrated this by submitting to two press conferences. ...We plead with all Southern Baptists to exercise Christian patience toward our new president. ... And let's honor his request for

Alvin Shackleford, center, was elected B&R *editor in September 1976. Eura Lannom, left, was serving as acting editor. Ralph Norton was executive secretary, Tennessee Baptist Convention, at the time.*

prayers on his behalf. ... He deserves our patience and our prayers."

Shackleford was editor when the TBC initiated its powerful mission outreach program by getting involved alongside the Foreign Mission Board's (International Mission Board) Partnership Missions thrust. Tennessee was the first "partner" in Partnership Missions. At the November 1980 TBC annual session, messengers approved a recommendation to "enter a relief project" with Upper Volta (Burkina Faso). One of the first projects would be in water conservation and drilling wells. Volunteers would be enlisted.

The plan was successful and led to partnerships with Venezuela and a dozen more. The role of the paper and involvement of the editor were paramount on successful mission work.

Other comments and editorial excerpts from Shackleford follow:

Inerrancy question needs answering, 1979 — The lasting issue which was raised at the Houston SBC was biblical inerrancy. The question raised and is still officially unanswered: Are there Southern Baptist leaders and professors who do not believe in the inerrancy of the Scriptures? ... Many Southern Baptist leaders — including our president, Adrian Rogers — do not want a "witch hunt." Let's not assume that all or any of our leaders and professors are "liberals."

Shackleford then suggested the appointment of a special committee and give it the power "to ask for clarification of any reports made by the trustees."

Letters needed, 1979 — The crisis in Iran is now into its seventh week. Fifty American citizens are still being held hostage. Diplomatic overtures, military or economic threats, and even the departure from the United States of the Shah have proven useless in attempts to secure the release of the hostages. May we make a request of you? ... We join with the Executive Board in asking that you, your friends, and church members send communications (to the Iranian Embassy) as soon as possible. How wonderful it would be if we could have as many letters sent to the Iranian Embassy as were sent to the Federal Communications Commission about an inaccurate petition (Madelyn O'Hair to the FCC). [Editors Shackleford, Allen, and Wilkey repeatedly wrote editorials refuting the O'Hair rumor, which still lives today.]

Dangerous trend, 1980 — For the first eighty years of its existence, the Southern Baptist Convention allowed its agencies "to go their own way" in securing financial support. Representatives from these organizations would pressure pastors to invite them to come, plead their case, and to take an offering. This resulted in inequalities: agencies with "heart appeal," such as foreign missions and child care, pulled the most money; representatives courted the larger, wealthier churches where there was the possibility of bigger offerings. Agencies with smaller budgets could not afford the effective fundraisers, and agencies spent a large portion of their funds on fund raising.

These frustrations led to the formation of the Cooperative Program in 1925. The concept is that Southern Baptists from all size churches contribute to the Convention's work through a central office, and these funds are distributed according to budgets approved by messengers to the state convention and the Southern Baptist Convention. Now there is rising a threat to the Cooperative Program ... that some agencies are looking for funds outside the Cooperative Program channel.

We believe the Cooperative Program must continue to be our major, if not only, method of supporting state and SBC agencies. To return to the method of individual agency solicitation would handicap the total ministry of our denomination.

William Tolbert: Baptist loss, 1980 — Baptists of the world have lost a great leader and friend with the assassination last Saturday of William R. Tolbert Jr., president of the Republic of Liberia. Tolbert was a Baptist pastor also, and was very active in international Baptist affairs. When the Baptist World Alliance held its 11th World Congress in 1965, Tolbert was elected president of the international organization.

His leadership in the role of BWA president brought to dramatic focus the international nature of the alliance. Baptists in the Third World cited his election as a refutal of the pagan propaganda that Christianity is merely a "white man's religion." We will miss the smiling face and the enthusiastic spirit of William Tolbert.

SBC leans toward "Conservative Right," 1980 — Generally the resolutions seemed to lean more toward the "conservative right" in moral, political, and theological issues than in recent conventions. The resolution on "doctrinal integrity" exhorted trustees of SBC seminaries and other agencies not to employ or continue employment of professors or staff who do not "believe in the divine inspiration of the whole Bible, the infallibility of the original manuscripts, and that the Bible is truth without any error."

We do not see (Bailey) Smith's election as one-sided endorsement of Biblical inerrancy. All six nominees are theological conservatives.

The pastor and church relationship, 1980 — The pastor-church relationship is in some ways like a marriage. It should not be entered into lightly. It must be based on a conviction that God's will is being followed. It must recognize that there are periods of "better, worse; richer, poorer; sickness, health." It must be entered into with a desire for permanency. The relationship between a church and its pastor is a sacred, God-given bond. Neither that pastor nor that church should tamper with that bond without anticipating God's judgment.

Praying for life-giving rain in Africa, 1985 — Let us commit ourselves to pray continually that God will send His life-giving rain on Africa. Pray that God will send a season of rain to Africa that will break the drought and that crops will be planted in time and will yield bountifully. Pray that our churches will make 1985 a year of prayer for Africa, because it will take months of rain to break the devastating drought — not temporarily but permanently.

Pray that God will use Southern Baptist missionaries as they minister to the physical need in the crisis, to bring a saving knowledge of Jesus Christ, the Living Water of Life, to thousands of people. Just imagine how God's answer to our prayers can be used to save physical life, to open doors to the saving Gospel, and to bring glory to God. Please commit yourself to pray for rain in Africa.

Historic commitment to education, 1985 — The importance of Christian higher education certainly has not diminished since this tremendous need was highlighted at the 1874 TBC organization. During the past 110 years, our churches and State Convention have benefited continually from the dedicated service of our TBC colleges. Our churches must continue to provide strong support, financial and otherwise, for our TBC colleges.

We urge pastors and church members to respond graciously to the challenge of the current endowment campaign for our three Tennessee Baptist colleges, to insure that these outstanding schools can continue to serve our churches, our denomination, and the Kingdom of God.

1985 SBC: good news, bad news, 1985 — The Dallas Convention produced what could be described as "good news, bad news" for Southern Baptists. Throughout our history, Southern Baptists have been known for their willingness to debate and to vote on any issue, and then to leave a convention in a spirit of unity because the body had spoken. Many left Dallas feeling that they did not have an opportunity to debate and vote on an issue which had been raised.

The major "good news" was the establishment of the Peace Committee. That action opens the door to our convention's best answer (humanly speaking) for reconciliation and healing. The committee has a tremendous assignment. Let us give them time and freedom to perform their convention-assigned task. The problems in our denomination have come over many years. These cannot be solved in a few months. It will take time and patience — and a mutual trust — along with that faith in each other and what God is doing in each other's lives which has led to the great ministry of our denomination. ... The committee must have our prayers and support. [While Shackleford and other editors asked Baptists to give the committee time to perform, SBC messengers had been given insufficient time to digest a very lengthy plan, at a late night hour and then to vote.]

Shackleford resigned the *B&R* editorship early in 1987. He was named vice president for public relations for the SBC Executive Committee in Nashville. The front page of the February 25 issue announced the move, and Shackleford used his Cicero's Comment column to explain his decision. His nomination had strong conservative opposition, but he was elected in a 32-26 vote.

His closing remarks revealed his courage and love for the paper and for Tennessee Baptists. "I am and will remain an active Tennessee Baptist. ... You have been very gracious in your comments and support during the past ten years. As my friends, I ask that you continue to pray for me, as you have when I was your editor. Pray that I will be given the opportunity of being a part of the healing of our denomination."

Charlie Warren became acting editor, and wrote an editorial page tribute to Shackleford for the March 25 issue. He praised

Shackleford for his fairness, openness, editorial stands, and staff relationships. Warren was "to supervise the office and oversee production of the *Baptist and Reflector*" until an editor was chosen. He served in that capacity from February until September when Wm. Fletcher Allen, Maryland/Delaware editor, was elected to replace Shackleford.

Warren represented the paper during the June SBC sessions with news coverage and a strong editorial about Convention actions, concluding, "Future historians can reflect on the significance of the 1987 SBC meeting. We simply say it was a good convention. More people seemed to enjoy themselves this year. There were more smiles and laughter. That in itself is an improvement over previous years."

B its of Biography, Alvin C. Shackleford — Native of Georgia; graduate of Mercer University; BA in journalism University of Georgia, and MDiv. from Southwestern Baptist Theological; married Tommye Griffith; two daughters; member of Southern Baptist Press Association, Baptist Public Relations Association; worked for Baptist General Convention of Texas; SBC Radio and Television Commission; Fort Worth *Star Telegram*; pastor of Glenloch Baptist Church, Franklin, Georgia; editor of *Indiana Baptist* eleven years; vice president for public relations, SBC Executive Committee; and later editor of *Mature Living* magazine. Shackleford died in an automobile accident July 23, 2000.

CHAPTER ELEVEN

Expansion in Missions
William Fletcher Allen
1987-98

There I was, veteran of staff positions with two Baptist state papers, being interviewed by a search committee to follow Al Shackleford as editor of the *Baptist and Reflector*. The interview must have gone well, because I accepted the committee's invitation and took office September 1, 1987. I came to Tennessee from my native South Carolina by way of a four-year "visit" with Maryland/Delaware.

Seventeen years as associate editor of South Carolina's *Baptist Courier* and four as editor of the *Baptist True Union* of Maryland/Delaware prepared me for the Tennessee position. Family and friends joined me in earnest prayer about the opportunity. I searched my heart for God's will — and found His answer. My wife and daughters agreed.

Now I have been retired since 1998 after serving eleven years as *B&R* editor, and by invitation writing a brief history of this venerable paper. Writing about other editors has taken many hours of research and composition — but that was the less difficult part of the task. When writing about yourself, the author usually tends to be more critical or more flattering. It's a matter of looking at yourself, with unbiased eyes. My task is to avoid both tendencies. As the only living former editor, I have the bonus of memories of contemporaries and my own experiences as I write this chapter of the paper.

Even with facts gathered through research, writing about former editors and their years with the *Baptist and Reflector* may be less lively than personal views of oneself. You gain the information from words on pages, or from current or recent life.

I have chosen to write this chapter in first person language rather than using the awkward third person style. So the personal noun "I" will appear often. A personal column, "One Word More," came with me. In the column I tried to reach readers with those things in life familiar to everyone — especially oriented to daily life experiences.

When I met with the TBC Executive Board June 26, 1987, I pledged to be honest and fair. I shared with board members that, "I believe the Bible, all of it. I believe everything in the Bible. I believe it is perfectly trustworthy. It is my authority for not only what I believe, but how I live."

I told the Board that I was [and still am] amazed at the enduring history of the paper and the strength of its editors.

Though my first issue came on September 9, that summer and fall provided many newsworthy events for the paper. In the July 1 issue just after I was elected editor, a front page *B&R* story reported that the Supreme Court struck down a Louisiana law mandating the teaching of creation science in the state's elementary and secondary schools when evolution also is taught. Chief Justice William Rehnquist and Justice Antonin Scalia charged that the majority had ruled in effect "that striking down a law approved by the democratically elected representatives of the people is no minor matter. The people of Louisiana, including those who are Christian fundamentalists, are quite entitled, as a secular matter, to have whatever scientific evidence there may be against evolution presented in their schools." Like other Baptist editors of that era, I realized that there was enough news, good and bad, to attract readers. New subscribers were important, but maintaining close ties with regular readers was highly important. News of Tennessee Baptists, including letters to the editor had top priority.

In the months that followed, events of impact were reported, such as — Associate Editor Charlie Warren accompanied 128 volunteers on a Partnership Mission to Venezuela, and reported 2,924 professions of faith and relief efforts for victims of gigantic mud slides and tornados, the editor recovered from major surgery, reports continued about the SBC Peace Committee, Memphis citizens voted in favor of pari-mutuel gambling, an SBC committee voted to sever ties with the Baptist Joint Committee on Public Affairs, Shelby County Baptist Association withdrew fellowship from Prescott Memorial Baptist Church for calling a woman as pastor, Nancy Hastings Sehested;

Wm. Fletcher Allen

Randall Lolley resigned as president of Southeastern Baptist Theological Seminary in disagreement with trustees and three executives joined him, long-time SBC executive Porter Routh died, TBC Convention messengers approved plans for a $4 million construction project for a new office building and renovation of current facility, WMU began centennial celebration, Associate Editor Warren resigned to edit *Home Life,* Conservative leaders met, Moderate group met, Rutherford and Williamson counties overwhelmingly voted against pari-mutuel gambling — and the editor wrote six editorials about the paper and its role, and several dealing with pari-mutuel gambling.

Those were eye-opening months. There were occasions when I wondered how my predecessors would have handled the situation. But they were "then," and now is now. I felt welcome, at home with Tennessee Baptists. One of those editorials was an introduction for readers, giving my pledge for openness and thorough reporting. It was a foundational declaration, a covenant for the best possible relationship between reader and paper. A brief summary follows:

"There are certain things we pledge to Tennessee Baptists," I wrote. "I will serve with integrity. The editorship of a Baptist newsjournal is no place for incompetency or dog leadership (where the leader makes no decision, and waits to see how the crowd moves). I pledge not to be a wugmump, no fence straddling. I will be fair. The paper will be the people's advocate. The *B&R* will never be used as a political tool. While I will not avoid controversy, I will not promote it nor delve into needless or non-Christian arguments. Many Baptists consider themselves editors, but the paper has only one, the elected one."

The editorial closed with an admission and a request, "In a sense, the *Baptist and Reflector* is the readers' paper. Some bad news inevitably will be included, but God's good news will be accentuated. We have made pledges to you, our readers. At the same time, there must come from you some responsibility to deal fairly, compassionately, honestly with your paper and its staff. You will want to read the paper habitually — to gain the news and resources provided weekly. Working together for Christ as Baptists of Tennessee, we will be bold, always on mission."

When I arrived at the *Baptist and Reflector*, there were two journalists on the staff — Charlie Warren, associate editor, and Connie Davis, assistant editor. After Warren resigned to edit *Home Life*, the paper replaced him with another experienced journalist, Lonnie Wilkey. He was a journalism graduate of the University of South Carolina and had writing experience from several Baptist entities.

With Wilkey and Davis on the staff, we had three journalists and Joy Jordan and Connie Umstead joined the staff at different times

Wm. Fletcher Allen, left, editor of the Baptist and Reflector, *receives a plaque from Lloyd Elder, president of the Baptist Sunday School Board (now LifeWay Christian Resources), Nashville, Jan. 17, 1991 at chapel at the Baptist Center. The plaque was in recognition of the action of E. E. Folk, editor of the paper, who gave space in his office to J.M. Frost, corresponding secretary of the board at its founding in 1891. The board was honoring friends and supporters during its centennial year.*

later on. Both continued careers as journalists after leaving the paper for other opportunities.

During my four years with the Maryland/Delaware Baptist Convention, the convention agreed with the Foreign Mission Board's request to take on Partnership Mission work with Burundi, and later with Rwanda. As a member of the fact-finding group, I rediscovered a deep love for people, nations, in need of physical and spiritual help. Those friendships developed into a deeper understanding of foreign missions, the countries, and the people.

So it's understandable that I would have a high priority for explaining and promoting Partnership Missions. Tennessee Baptists' long involvement with the program was a strong influence in my desire to join the Tennessee Baptist Convention as its editor.

In my role as editor those eleven years, Partnership Missions was (and is) one of my greatest spiritual joys. I went, worked, came home, and reported to Tennessee Baptists about their partnerships with Venezuela, Philippines, Chile, Costa Rica, Canada, Poland, and Rio de Janeiro.

Return trips to some proved even more beneficial for reports through the *B&R* and in person before churches — and enhancing the program throughout the Tennessee Baptist family. On a personal note, there were two mission trips to Australia, one with thirty East Tennessee Baptists, and one as leader of a group from ClearView Baptist Church, Franklin, and a trip to Ukraine as well. Partnership Missions is a life-changing strategy with eternal results for both partners. The longstanding partnership with Michigan Baptists was the source of scores of news stories and features as churches and individuals worked together.

As in previous years, world changes continued at home and abroad during my service with the paper. Other editors dealt with problems within the denomination nationally and in Tennessee. Some of the problems were similar to those of today; others were peculiar to the times and tenor of situations.

Certainly near the top of the list were difficulties in producing a practical and helpful paper on limited budgets. From the beginning, costs of mailing and production were constant. Production of the paper included costs of newsprint and printing. It must be mentioned here that a second class postage permit regulates denominational papers and some other categories of mail. A limit is

Jim Henry, left, Southern Baptist Convention president and pastor, First Baptist Church, Orlando, Fla., receives a copy of the new book, Contending for the Right to Know, *a history of the Southern Baptist Press Association from Wm. Fletcher Allen, editor,* Baptist and Reflector, *at the 1996 SBC annual meeting as SBPA president Bill Webb of Missouri looks on. Webb is editor of the* Word and Way *of Missouri.*

placed on the amount of advertising used, and postal authorities have complete control over these costs. Rates are increased sometimes after the papers' budgets are in place.

Reader interest fluctuated also from the beginning with R.B.C. Howell's first issue in 1835. Periodically editors have had to remind Tennessee Baptists of the importance of the paper in the life of churches and individuals. This problem persists, and is more prevalent now because of electronically produced information — such as Internet and e-mail. But despite such problems, most of our Baptist papers survived; some flourished through turmoil, and others consolidated. In fact, the *Baptist and Reflector* has at least a dozen Baptist papers in its background.

John D. Freeman, editor of the *B&R* 1925-33 and later TBC executive secretary, wrote an incisive opinion piece in 1959 for the 125th anniversary issue. In it he addressed *"Baptist and Reflector* and Doctrinal Strength." He closed with this belief;

"It will be difficult for one not familiar with the development of our Baptist life during the past two centuries, to appreciate the part the denominational press played during the early period of our great growth in unifying us and giving direction to our doctrinal life."

An article in the January 3, 1990 issue, suggested seven key points in Baptist heritage. The writer, Art Toalston, said, "All

The August 16, 1995 issue featured the 160th anniversary of the newsjournal which could be celebrated on Baptist and Reflector Day, *Aug. 20.*

denominations have shortcomings and sad chapters in their history, including Southern Baptists. But despite our differences and even spats, there is much to be said for being a Southern Baptist."

He listed seven marks of Southern Baptists — Lion-heartedness, mentioning persecuted Anabaptists of the 1500s; fervency of freedom, worldwide vision, missions mobilization, beginnings that keep us humble, cooperative effectiveness, and global partnering.

On the opposite page, Foreign Mission Board representative Mike Creswell wrote about the celebratory events of religious freedom that exploded after the "rusty" Iron Curtain crumbled and nations were loosed from communism's brutal force.

In addition to a strong dedication to Partnership Missions, there are at least six other areas of work that are memorable points for me — (1) discovering readers who had been reading the paper the longest period of time, (2) publishing history of Southern Baptist Press Association, (3) hiring Lonnie Wilkey to the *B&R* staff, (4) the questionable firing of newsmen Al Shackleford and Dan Martin from the SBC Executive Committee, (5) participating in the 100th anniversary in 1997 of the founding of Zionism in Israel, and (6) continuing to help produce and mail tapes and *B&R* news to Tennessee Baptists with severe eyesight problems.

Of course scores of major happenings took place among Tennessee Baptists and elsewhere in the world during the 1987-98 era, some of which are mentioned on these pages. Some highlights follow:

Who has read the B&R longer? — In 1993 the staff began a search for longtime readers, and announced the plan early that spring. We asked readers of long years to write letters to us, telling their stories. The letters may be published some day as a special part of Baptist history. At least twenty readers responded with fifty years of faithful reading. A few exceeded sixty. Two had been avid for seventy-five and seventy years. But the champions were readers for eighty years — Beatrice Farrow Rives and Bonita Sharp Holt, both of First Baptist Church, Jefferson City. When I interviewed them, they admitted they were still faithful readers.

Why be involved in publishing the history of an editors' group? — The history, *Contending for the Right to Know*, is an effort to preserve some of the major events in Southern Baptist life from 1895 until 1995. Later that history will need updating. Led by E.E.

Folk, *B&R* editor, the group was established for editors of Baptist State papers for fellowship, workshops, and discussing methods for becoming more effective. The book is entertaining and interesting — and a few copies are still available.

Another journalist on the staff — As the Tennessee Baptist Convention grows in numbers, ministries, and events, churches, associations, and individuals need all the viable information, including features, facts and figures, and editorials. Experienced Baptist journalists are necessary to provide news, features, reports, and editorials for Tennessee churches and individuals. With partnerships still growing and along with disaster relief and developing new strategies and plans, experienced journalists are needed. Lonnie Wilkey proved his worth immediately.

SBC executive committee's firing two newsmen, Shackleford and Martin — While this event did not touch directly most Tennessee Baptists, the overall effect was crucial. Under the leadership of the two men, Baptist Press and Southern Baptists were well represented to the world and nation by professional journalists. Al Shackleford, former *B&R* editor who became vice president of public relations for the SBC Executive Committee, was fired in early 1990 along with Dan Martin, news director for Baptist Press. The Executive Committee held its meeting behind closed doors and did not give reasons for the firings. Support for the two journalists and for the committee was substantial. Despite efforts to prevent the action, the two were released. However, the major "cause" was growing disapproval by conservative forces over news handling by the two journalists. As a result, the reputation of Baptist Press suffered. The Southern Baptist Press Association met and vowed support of the two, and promised to keep a close watch on the news service, and to use other news sources as needed.

The founding of Zionism — In 1996-97, the Israeli government celebrated the beginning of Zionism — the birth of a plan for a Jewish homeland. I was one of six journalists chosen to report on a portion of the two-year event. Theodor Herzl, an Austrian citizen, was the "father" of the idea. Highlights of the reporting were remembering that the United States, by action of President Harry Truman, voted in favor of the declaration of the new state of Israel in 1948 — and visiting Independence Hall in Tel Aviv, the building where Jewish leaders declared the re-birth of Israel in the homeland.

Some editorial excerpts:

Living by principle of freedom, losing a job, July 25, 1990 — We feel sadness for all those involved in the July 17 affair (firing of Shackleford and Martin) — the men on "trial," Executive Committee members, those barred from the meeting, and every Southern Baptist. The anger expressed by so many is understandable — but we can overcome even this and work and pray for a brighter future, unhindered by closed meetings. That future will be well lighted by freedom which Baptists know well and which cannot be snuffed out.

Taking up the banner for truth and right, 1995 — So in 1995, we must be judged by the challenges we define for ourselves, rather than the conflicts we avoid. The paper must be an instrument to help chart the path of understanding. There is a basic unity out there for Baptists. We must find it. It is no false claim that today's *Baptist and Reflector* is the only authentic voice for Tennessee Baptists. We must always provide that forum for the pursuit of truth and right.

Passions of the world aren't always healthy, 1995 — What the world still needs is Christ's medicine, the pure and undiluted Word, the salvation of our Lord, the love that forgives. ... Southern Baptists must replace the passions of the world with the Passion of Christ. If we don't, someone else will, and God will enable whom He chooses to do it without us. Make no mistake. If Southern Baptists are to make a difference of magnitude, first we will include each other in love and forgiveness. That lifestyle is a two-way street.

Tough, clean, committed, challenge for 1992 — In this new year, pastors and laity alike are challenged by our Lord. A news story tells us that Americans now have the lowest level of confidence in the clergy than ever before. Moral pollution is rising on all sides. Honesty in the marketplace and in politics is ebbing. But the challenge of Christian strategy is not to exclude the outsiders, the outcast, but to minister with toughness, pure motive, and commitment that surpasses that which is modeled by the world.

The never ending task, reporting to the readers, 1993 — To build on past achievements calls for our greatest cooperative effort. The work will become more difficult. We pray that the day has not passed when Baptists are recognized as people who try to do good, rather than becoming known as tepid, sluggish, quarrelsome, worldly do-gooders.

Call to commitment, Cooperative Program Day, 1991 — Historically the Cooperative Program is a proven force in regular, systematic, missions giving by churches all across the TBC and

Wm. Fletcher Allen, editor of the Baptist and Reflector, *is thanked on his retirement in the March 25, 1998 issue.*

Southern Baptist Convention. Where there is not a concerted effort to give sacrificially and cooperatively, individual churches may resort to gimmicks, which in the medical profession would be called quackery.

It is shameful that Christians have to be cajoled and begged to do what Christ already has commanded. Do we indeed love the lost people of Tennessee and the rest of the world?

And now, some advice for grandchildren, 1998 — Listen to Jesus. Begin right now to walk with your hand in His hand. I have learned a lot because I have also listened to Jesus, and I have let Him show me the guidelines for my life. Most of all, I'll tell you that God's love for me, and my love for God and for people has helped me be what God intended me to be. I hope you will always love God, your family, and your country. Be proud to be an American, and try to help make our country great.

My decade with the *Baptist and Reflector*, despite inevitable bumps in the road, was a work of love. I loved my job — because I knew God's will for me. The staff blessed me, as did people from hundreds of churches and associations, leaders, and families. Just a year after my arrival, the *B&R* benefited as we occupied new and spacious quarters in the Baptist Center's 1989 expansion. We could breathe!

I am the only editor who has served with three Tennessee Baptist executive directors — Tom Madden, D.L. Lowrie, and James Porch — and I learned from each of them.

Three additional innovations were made during the Allen era — (1) word-processing that was greatly enhanced with the advent of computers for staff and production use, (2) the frequent use of color print and photographs, and newfound capability to coordinate page layouts, design new formats, and (3) instituting "Families Matter," a regular column produced by Paul Barkley, counselor and former Baptist pastor, and other family related material.

Now, even as this book is being prepared for publication, our world continues to be greatly disturbed and disrupted. We daily live among tragedies —
- increasing numbers of lost people
- natural disasters such as hurricanes Katrina and Rita
- global warming

- the abomination of same-sex "marriage"
- petty but debilitating bickering among politicians at every level
- wars in Iraq and Afghanistan
- bloody distrust between religions
- labeling and constant bickering among Baptists and in political groups
- ill-mannered relationships, child abuse, proliferating pornography
- schools teaching the theory of evolution and excluding the biblical truth of creation
- threats of nuclear conflicts
- the menace of drug addiction
- widespread lack of respect
- abortion of babies (in particular partial birth abortions)
- the blight of AIDS
- ridiculous rulings by judges who ignore laws and the Constitution.

I haven't named them all.

But in reviewing our own history, we see that evil was always among us even though God prevails. We also realize the great and good accomplishments of our God. And knowing that this venerable and dedicated Baptist newspaper has survived because God raised up leaders with profound love of Christ and His Word, and with desire to give the good news of his work in Tennessee — we pledge anew to honor our heritage.

B its of Biography, William Fletcher Allen — Born in Darlington County, South Carolina, July 1, 1931, to Frederick and Marguerite Allen; graduate in English, History, and Journalism at Furman University, Greenville, South Carolina; married to Betty Frances Fink 1954 (deceased March 2003); four daughters; Korean War service veteran; employment with newspapers, college, industry, and three Baptist State papers; president of Southern Baptist Press Association, 1992; vice president of Tennessee Baptist Convention, 1999-2000; oversight editor of SBPA for *Contending for the Right to Know;* author of family history, *Half a Dozen Assorted;* cousin W.C. Allen edited the *Baptist Courier* 1935-40, and cousin Clifton J. Allen served as an editor with the Baptist Sunday School Board (LifeWay Christian Resources) forty years.

CHAPTER TWELVE

Into a New Century
Lonnie H. Wilkey
1998-

Six months after Wm. Fletcher Allen retired as editor of the *Baptist and Reflector*, a search committee selected Lonnie Wilkey as his successor. His election was announced at an Executive Board meeting. It was a logical and sound move. Wilkey had served as associate editor for ten years. He was well acquainted with Tennessee Baptists and as an experienced journalist, he had served six years prior as director of public communications for the SBC's Education Commission located in Nashville. He had worked in the Press Room at several SBC annual sessions. He had served on the staffs of two Baptist colleges, and was a graduate of the University of South Carolina School of Journalism, and a South Carolinian.

With Connie Davis already on board as assistant editor, the paper would have two journalists to continue the work. Both were known as excellent reporters and news writers. Both also were capable photographers. Wilkey served as interim editor for six months before his election as editor.

Herbert Higdon, chairman of the search committee, said, "As interim, Lonnie Wilkey demonstrated his ability to be editor of the *Baptist and Reflector* and in that capacity he did an outstanding job. ... His dedication is to Tennessee Baptists and his concern is to convey the news that is important to our constituency."

Wilkey has continued the paper's efforts to gain more sub-scribers and to operate with efficiency and dedication. He promoted special editions in support of programs such as Partnership

Missions and other entities. One of his strengths is his dedicated support of missions — in Tennessee and with partnerships.

In his first editorial September 23, 1998, he let readers know that the paper wanted and needed the support of all Tennessee Baptists. "We have to work harder to increase circulation so we can deal with postage and printing cost increases. ... Our primary concern will be stories that feature concerns of interest to Tennessee Baptists, such as family matters, how to make your church more effective in reaching people for Christ, and much more. We will continue to share national Southern Baptist news of interest ... be assured that I pledge to always do my best and to be as fair as humanly possible while seeking God's will for my life and the paper."

Lonnie Wilkey

In May 1999 Davis was named news editor, replacing the associate editor post. Wilkey explained, "Connie Davis is uniquely qualified for this role. She brings a wealth of experience to the position. Her long tenure with the paper has enabled her to develop relationships that will prove valuable as we work together reporting the work of Tennessee Baptists."

A strong letters page was continued, and comic strips produced by Baptist artists began to appear as a regular feature.

Wilkey has proven to be a determined foe against gambling in Tennessee. He took aim at the gambling industry editorially and in news and feature stories. As the Tennessee legislature approved a statewide referendum on gambling, he increased pressure on the pages of the paper, and did not hesitate to name legislators who persistently and openly approved the referendum and gambling. Wilkey and his staff spearheaded publication of a well-planned booklet for Tennessee Baptists, *Keep Tennessee Gambling Free*. He solicited articles from a variety of sources and gained followers in the fight. Eventually, however, the legislature approved the referendum and Tennesseans voted to permit a state-run lottery by a large margin. *B&R* editors for decades had fought against legalized gambling and its evils.

He developed his own style in editorial writing — some folksy, some personal, and others touched on subjects and events that affected Tennessee Baptists as a body. In years following his election, the paper has had to report on different events and situations — some positive, some negative. Wilkey addressed many of these editorially, such as — September 11, 2001, in New York; his bout

September 26, 2001, issue which featured the reporting of Connie Davis Bushey on Tennessee Baptist Disaster Relief efforts in New York City following 9/11.

with cancer; controversy within the Tennessee Baptist Convention; how to deal with conflict; rulings on the Pledge of Allegiance; homosexuality in the ministry; Disaster Relief; mission trips to Rio de Janeiro; prayerwalking in Iowa; and issues concerning Belmont University and Carson-Newman College. An editorial about the Baptist World Alliance and the Southern Baptist Convention also drew attention.

From its beginning, Wilkey has been an advocate and vocal supporter of True Love Waits, the SBC program for sexual abstinence before marriage. Even now the *B&R* keeps the issue before the people. Another innovation is a regular column written by Tennessee Baptist women — for families. He also began to utilize guest columnists to write on timely topics and began a new column entitled, "From Both Sides of the Pulpit," written by Johnnie Godwin. This column looks at issues churches face from the perspective of one who has been a pastor and also has sat in the pew as a layman.

Certainly readers will remember the excellent coverage of the September 11, 2001, terrorists' attack in New York that demolished both towers of the World Trade Center. *B&R* News Editor Connie Davis accompanied scores of Tennessee Baptists in disaster relief. Davis was with the workers at Ground Zero. Her photography and word portraits carried the story firsthand to readers. Coverage continued in subsequent issues.

Both journalists continue firsthand coverage of mission trips by TBC and church groups. The October 6, 2004 issue records several pages of news and photos by Lonnie Wilkey of mission work in Rio de Janeiro.

Let's look at excerpts from some of Lonnie Wilkey's editorials:

Christians should beware, form opinions on news, 2000 — I have mixed emotions about the plight of six-year-old Elian Gonzalez, the Cuban boy who was rescued off the Florida coast after he and his mother attempted to escape from Cuba. His mother died and Elian was placed in the custody of some distant relatives living in Florida. His father wants him returned to Cuba. ... Some congressmen want to grant Elian American citizenship. I don't believe anyone should be granted citizenship on the whim of Congress. ... I can only imagine how the father must feel. Elian should be reunited with his father and family in Cuba. We need to trust God that someday Elian will learn about and come to know Jesus Christ as his Lord and Savior. (Editor's note: Elian eventually returned to Cuba.)

What has become of personal responsibility? — Christians and churches in particular need to teach the importance of personal responsibility. We need to teach our children that choices they make now can affect them for a lifetime — whether it be smoking, drinking alcohol, or having sex before marriage. And what's more, they need to be aware they are responsible for the consequences of their actions. The idea of personal responsibility is biblical.

One size does not fit all, 2000 — I get amused when I read an advertisement about a piece of clothing that says, "one size fits all." People of all sizes may be able to put on that piece of clothing. It will be loose on some people, tight on others, and on some people it may fit just right. But it really does not fit all. The same can be said of blanket statements. ... We have at least one Southern Baptist seminary president who is known to have Calvinistic leanings. Calvinists generally believe in pre-determined election of the saved. This seminary president is a leading conservative. Does that mean every conservative is a Calvinist? No. ... We need to be wary of making blanket statements. ... I pray for the day we will quit classifying people as moderates or conservatives. ... The only blanket I want to be lumped with is that of "Christian." God holds that blanket and it certainly is big enough to include everyone.

In a personal column in May 2001, Wilkey shared with readers that a routine physical examination revealed cancer of his colon. He expressed his faith and deep belief in prayer. A month later he reported on the surgery and appreciation for the many prayers and expressions of continuing support:

Why me? Better still, why not me? — "I have no idea what the eventual outcome will be as to radiation or chemotherapy," he wrote. "My personal preference would be to forego any of those, but ultimately that will be up to my doctors. Only one thing is certain. I know without a shadow of doubt that the same God who was with me through the diagnosis and surgery, will be with me through the remainder of the process."

God still extends His grace and love, September 19, 2001 — We are not close to where we need to be as a country in our relationship with God. But after last week (September 11 terrorist attack in

New York) I sense more people are coming to the realization that we need God. I cannot remember in my lifetime the numerous references made by the secular media and government leaders about trusting in God and praying for our country. On September 11 our Executive Board was meeting. Board President Verlon Moore cut to the heart of the matter as only he could, "It is time to quit singing 'God Bless America' and begin living a life that He can bless."

We need only one side, one Boss — God, 2001 — We do not need sides in the Tennessee Baptist Convention. There should be only side and one Boss, God. What will our actions convey to people inside and outside our Convention (annual meeting)? Will our actions speak so loud that the outside world does not hear us when we try to share the Gospel of Christ?

Judge's ruling may have awakened everyone, 2002 — Like most Americans I was shocked and then angry when I learned that a federal appeals court judge in California had ruled that public school recitation of the Pledge of Allegiance was unconstitutional because the pledge contains the phrase "under God." ... While Americans from all walks of life have expressed outrage about the decision in California, are we really surprised? Have we not seen it coming? We cannot continue to live with our heads buried in the sand.

The *B&R* of September 17, 2003, celebrated the 25th year of Disaster Relief in action. — For twenty-five years Tennessee Baptists have rallied around Disaster Relief. Volunteers have stepped forward when called. We have sent Tennessee Baptists all over the world, not for their personal glory, but to bring glory and honor to the One in whose name we minister, Jesus Christ. ... We cannot rest on our laurels. Until Jesus returns, disasters will continue to plague Tennessee Baptists and we must be ready to respond.

Lines are being drawn; will ours be by pencil or Sharpie? 2004 — Lines are being drawn in the debate over same-sex "marriages" in our state and in our nation. The biblical and traditional definition of marriage (a union between one man and one woman) is being challenged on many fronts. Courts have dropped the ball and allowed the lines to be blurred. ... Lines are being drawn. Will our lines be drawn by a pencil that can be erased or with a Sharpie (God's Word) that will not fade. Christians can make a difference, but only if we want to. And in the May 26 issue — As Christians we

Current staff of the Baptist and Reflector *with a combined 100 years of service include, from left, Susie Edwards, Betty Williams, Mary Nimmo, and Connie Davis Bushey.*

can choose to ignore this, but in doing so we are choosing to ignore God's Word, thus risking His wrath upon us. We must take a stand for morality and not be afraid to say homosexuality is a sin and it is not a lifestyle that should be given societal approval.

Baptist World Alliance deserves a better fate, 2003 — The Baptist World Alliance has become a victim in the ongoing squabble between the Southern Baptist Convention and the Cooperative Baptist Fellowship. The BWA is a global organization composed of 206 member bodies, representing more than 43 million baptized believers around the world. The Cooperative Baptist Fellowship is an organization of Baptists who say they have been disenfranchised by the Southern Baptist Convention. ... The BWA is caught in the middle. CBF leaders have asked to join the organization and SBC leaders are opposed, feeling the membership process is flawed. The end result is that the SBC is going to cut our annual allocation to BWA by thirty percent.

Many of them (BWA member bodies) live in poverty-stricken countries and cannot support the BWA, as they would like to. Our cut will have a significant impact on the BWA which is already struggling financially. ... I am not calling on Southern Baptists to openly embrace the CBF, but we should at least have a truce, so the two groups can sit down together under the umbrella of the BWA without throwing darts at each other. ... The BWA has worked well since 1905 and has served all Baptists effectively.

The cover of the September 14, 2005 issue of the Baptist and Reflector, *which focused on Tennessee Baptist Disaster Relief efforts for victims of Hurricane Katrina which struck the Gulf Coast in late August of 2005.*

Lonnie Wilkey came to The Editor's Chair in 1998, and now has completed seven years. We anticipate continued progress and success in providing for Tennessee Baptists the best paper in the SBC family.

As we close the pages of this book, Lonnie Wilkey's leadership with the *Baptist and Reflector* is ongoing. Issues now extant will continue. Expansion of Disaster Relief and Partnership Missions is certain. Relationships among Tennessee Baptists, moderate and conservative are yet to be determined. Continuation of its mission for witness, mission, and evangelism on all fronts by every Tennessee Baptist entity is without question.

The *Baptist and Reflector* continues to provide the good news of the gospel of Jesus Christ — and how and where that mission will be implemented. The printed page, as always, will be the best informational friend of Tennessee Baptists. Several staffers with long tenures continue to serve with Lonnie Wilkey — Connie Davis Bushey and Susie Edwards, each with twenty years; Betty Williams, forty-six years; Mary Nimmo, fourteen years; and Marcia Knox, twenty years with the Tennessee Baptist Convention in media work, and a newcomer to the staff. Williams recently announced she will retire effective December 30, 2005. Enabled by a staff with such glittering years of experience, the paper moves into the future with pride and promise.

Bits of Biography, Lonnie H. Wilkey — Native of Marietta, South Carolina, born in 1958; journalism graduate University of South Carolina; held public relations positions with North Greenville College, Tigerville, and Baptist College at Charleston (now Charleston Southern University), South Carolina; director of communications for the SBC's Education Commission; served on news staff of SBC annual sessions several years; news editor for the *Northwest Sentinel,* Travelers Rest, South Carolina; president of Association of State Baptist Editors; married to Joyce Day of Greenville, South Carolina; two children — Joanna, 20, and Daniel, 16; joined *B&R* staff 1988.

Epilogue:
Sitting at the Desk

Old movies or novels often referred to the newspaper office or editor's desk. We could envision a sign on the desk, reminding the viewer that, "The Buck Stops Here." Maybe that originated with President Harry Truman. The adage is true and apropos, especially for wordsmiths, editors. Another axiom tells us that the customer is always right. Baptist editors might wink and add, "Well, almost always."

Did you ever pause to think how vulnerable are editors of today? The disgruntled "customer" can drive over to the editor's office, call by telephone, send an e-mail, or discuss the editor's faults with friends at coffee time. The old-timers who sat in the editor's chair were often secluded, not by design but by life's realities — no telephones for that first group, no automobiles, no "next day" postal service.

They may have ridden horseback, traveled by buggy, sent and received mail over a span of two weeks' delivery. Today we can hop a jet plane, fly to Washington or Boston, and return the same day. If necessary, we can drive a comfortable automobile to Memphis or Kingsport in a few hours. We can reach almost any Tennessee Baptist by telephone or e-mail in minutes.

I honor them, admire them. Though they could not quickly or easily communicate with constituents, they obeyed God and carried out the mission — just as we do. Through days and perhaps years, they did not knuckle under to hardships. They were optimistic and sometimes opportunistic. Don't forget that, above all, they loved God and knew their Call. In my hours among the aged records of old volumes, I realized the editors viewed life through rose-colored glasses. This is to say, they knew reality of each dreadful or beautiful situation — but the Christlike optimism reminded them always to see victory, and to press on toward the goal.

We who have served with help from modern conveniences must practice that same stubborn stick-to-itiveness.

Let's go back to The Desk — when you began reading in the Prologue.

Sitting at The Desk does not guarantee success or an easy ride for any editor. I recall sitting at the editor's desk on my first day with the *Baptist and Reflector*. When I first saw it on an interview visit to Brentwood, the desk was covered by papers and notes and just plain stuff. But on this first day, it was clean, polished. Was it a throne? A closer look revealed blemishes on the desktop — as though someone had used it for a carpenter's bench. There were dents permanently engraved into that beautiful cherry wood desk.

Poor editor, I thought, he must have had a second job as carpenter. Or, did he bang his fist or head on the desk when things went wrong. I don't know the answer even now. But I do know that I revered The Desk, even with the blemishes. It reminded me of the heritage I would join, and the blessings involved. Quickly it became the desk — for me.

That desk, now a partner of Lonnie Wilkey, is an emblem of honor, a messenger of the turmoil and victories set aside for faithful wordsmiths. I'd like to think that Howell sat behind the desk, Graves, Folk, and the rest. In truth, it's only thirty or forty years old. But it wears well!

We've tried to unfold the story of the first 170 years of the *Baptist and Reflector* in a different way. I have not uncovered some dark mystery or poignant story. I have tried to tell readers that this paper is real, alive, and moving forward as years pass. This paper provides what you need to know about Tennessee Baptists. The editors and the paper are almost twins, each the replica of the other.

Perhaps we have piqued or stirred up renewed interest in this official and friendly newsjournal. And maybe Tennessee Baptists will appreciate more the hard work of their paper from 1835 until today. R.B.C. Howell would revel in that, but he would be modest about applause!

We have given you a glimpse into the distant past, carried you through the middle years, and brought you up to the present. It is refreshing to look back — to see how our Tennessee Baptist family developed, often riding on the pages of a newsjournal that has eschewed glamour and discord, while serving Tennessee Baptists.

There are no star politicians, movie people, or athletes to help us promote the paper. Besides the paper itself, which always stands up for your approval, our best promoters and friends are Baptists. They are Tennessee Baptists who want to know about Baptist life — families on volunteer missions, disaster relief, Bible study, in-depth training, and you name it. The paper never feeds the reader with gruel — its mainstay is steak and potatoes.

As I researched pertinent materials for this book, I lugged bound volumes and other books from shelf to desk to table and back again. I learned that these pages are heavy, *really heavy!* I share this with you, the reader — The *Baptist and Reflector* is heavy, heavy with news about you and your church friends, about God's truth, put on pages and sent to all corners of our Tennessee. And someday, others will be writing another history of the paper and the pages will be heavy. Those "others" may be just like some of us, dwarfs on the shoulders of giants.

Read with me, something attributed to Bernard of Chartres, twelfth century —

"We are like dwarfs on the shoulders of giants, so that we can see more than they, and things at a greater distance, not by virtue of any sharpness of sight on our part, or any physical distinction, but because we are carried high and raised up by their giant size."

Now then, didn't you enjoy these pages of "heavy" stuff? The Desk may not be around 170 years from today — but we believe the *Baptist and Reflector* and its editors will be here! Do you realize that the bicentennial is only thirty years from now? See you then!

Wm. Fletcher Allen, erstwhile editor
Franklin, Tennessee
October 2005